To - Cathy to remember our
Australian Christmas 2005.
Erna

W9-CJP-616

modern classics BOOK 1

To - Cathy to remember our
Australian Christmas 2005.
Erna

about the author

Donna Hay is an Australian-based food stylist, author, food writer and magazine editor. Her most recent cookbook, *off the shelf*, published with HarperCollins, was a bestseller, and *donna hay* magazine, launched in 2001 with News Magazines, is a continuing popular success. She also has a weekly Australia-wide newspaper column and is well known for the four cookbooks she produced for *marie claire* – *marie claire cooking*, *marie claire dining*, *marie claire food fast* and *marie claire flavours* (published internationally as *The New Cook*, *New Entertaining*, *New Food Fast* and *Flavours*, respectively) – which have brought her global success.   Awards and nominations to date: for *off the shelf*, Gourmand World Cookbook Awards (Spain) – Best Design Book in English. For *food fast*, Jacob's Creek World Food Media Awards (Aus) – Silver Award, Best Soft Cover Recipe Book 2001; The Vittoria Australian Food Writers' Awards (Aus) – Food Media Club Australia Award for Best Soft Cover Recipe Book 2001. For *flavours*, The Guild of Food Writers Awards 2000 (UK) – Cookery Book of the Year; Glenfiddich Award (UK) – Best Cook Book 2001; James Beard Foundation/Kitchen Aid Book Awards (USA) – nominee for Best Food Photography 2001. For *dining*, Jacob's Creek World Food Media Awards (Aust) – Gold Award – Best Soft Cover Recipe Book 1999; Australian Food Writers' Award 1999 (Aust) for Best Soft Cover Recipe Book. For *cooking*, International Association of Culinary Professionals Cookbook Awards (USA) (formerly the Julia Child Cookbook Awards) – The Design Award 1998.

thank you

Vanessa Holden – what an extraordinary gal, what a creative director, what an inspiration. The lovely Lucy T–W – my food loves your beautiful words, and so do I. Con Poulos – what a joy it is to work with you, and what beautiful pictures you take. My adorable kitchen chicks, Kate Murdoch, Sonia Greig, Briget Palmer and Justine Poole – you keep me laughing, working and laughing some more; big, big thanks for the long hours and unflagging dedication. Didee Bull – you keep the business and my life running like a dream, not the potential disaster zone it could be. My tops of the props, Paula Berge, Heidi Castles and Sibella Court – for the wonderful treasures you hunt out.   Shona Martyn, Brian Murray, Christine Farmer and all the team at HarperCollins – for your endless support and incredible wisdom.   Billy, my wonderful partner – so understanding, so easy to love. Mum, Dad, my sisters, nieces and friends – for being there. My faithful and hardworking magazine staff – for producing perfect mags while this book was happening in the middle of it all.   Anticos Fruitworld, Demcos Seafoods, Paddington Fresh Foods and Broadway Fresh Foods – for your fantastic produce, advice and service. Shelly of Mud Australia, Ruth McMillan, Royal Doulton, Wedgwood, Wheel and Barrow, Orrefors Kosta Boda, Pillivuyt @ Hale Imports, Le Creuset, Chefs' Warehouse, The Bay Tree, Accoutrement, Simon Johnson and Peppergreen Trading Co – for your fabulous props. Tony Lee and Smeg Appliances, Profiline cookware, KitchenAid and Sunbeam – for my kitchen equipment.

HarperCollins*Publishers*

First published in Australia in 2002
by HarperCollins*Publishers* Pty Limited
ABN 36 009 913 517
A member of the HarperCollins*Publishers* (Australia) Pty Limited Group
www.harpercollins.com.au

Copyright © Donna Hay 2002
Design copyright © Vanessa Holden/ad +d pty ltd 2002
Photographs copyright © Con Poulos 2002

The right of Donna Hay, Vanessa Holden and Con Poulos to be identified as the moral rights author, designer and photographer of this work has been asserted by them in accordance with the *Copyright Amendment (Moral Rights) Act 2000 (Cth)*.

This book is copyright.
Apart from any fair dealing for the purposes of private study, research, criticism or review, as permitted under the *Copyright Act*, no part may be reproduced by any process without written permission.
Inquiries should be addressed to the publishers.

HarperCollins*Publishers*
25 Ryde Road, Pymble, Sydney, NSW 2073, Australia
31 View Road, Glenfield, Auckland 10, New Zealand
77–85 Fulham Palace Road, London W6 8JB, United Kingdom
Hazelton Lanes, 55 Avenue Road, Suite 2900, Toronto, Ontario M5R 3L2
and 1995 Markham Road, Scarborough, Ontario M1B 5M8, Canada
10 East 53rd Street, New York NY 10022, USA

National Library of Australia Cataloguing-in-Publication data:

Hay, Donna.
   Modern classics. Book 1.
   Includes index.
   ISBN 0 7322 7108 8.
   1. Cookery. I. Title
641.5

Cover photograph: Beef and red wine pies. For recipe, see page 158
Film by Colorwize Studios, Adelaide, South Australia
Produced by Phoenix Offset on 157gsm Chinese Matt
Printed in China

6 5 4 3 2 1   02 03 04 05

modern classics book 1

donna hay

photography by con poulos

HarperCollins*Publishers*

contents

introduction

Like a lot of people I know of my generation, I treasure the commonsense kind of basic cookery books that were given to us by our mothers and grandmothers, and I'll often use them for an inspirational starting point when I'm thinking of old things to cook in a new way. I also love to see a new dish with incredible staying power making its mark as a next-generation classic. And that's what the *modern classics* are a combination of – an update of the timeless classics and an establishment of some new ones.

What macaroni cheese was to me, risotto will be to the children of today when they become the adults doing the cooking in the future. But who wants to see as formative and influential a meal as macaroni cheese fall off the everyday meal agenda? Certainly not me. That's why recipes for a new-look macaroni cheese and a step-by-step guide to making risotto both feature in *modern classics book 1*, along with delicious juxtapositions such as spaghetti and meatballs and pad thai, coleslaw and tabouli, pea and ham soup and laksa. They're all there, as well as the basics you'll need no matter whether you're cooking in retro or future classic mode – how to make stock, cook rice, make pastry or a mash.

In updating the classics, I've taken into account the different ways we cook and eat food in modern life, and the new kinds of ingredients that are now readily available. (More information about ingredients and basic recipes marked with an asterisk* can be found in the glossary.) My aim was to present commonsense cookery in a modern way, so that mothers, fathers, grandmothers and grandfathers would have something practical and inspiring to give the next generation of young adults as they leave home, and enjoy a cooking revival in their own kitchens. There's a sweet version – *modern classics book 2* – on the way, too.

Here's to a whole new generation of passionate cooks, and to a newly inspired current one!

Donna

soup

steaming
warming
reviving

I love the simplicity of soup. So easy to make, so great to eat. You can serve a little as a starter or a big bowl as a hearty meal in itself. You can eat it to warm up or to settle down. It works as an everyday meal or as part of a special spread. My rule is to always make more than I need. People inevitably want another bowlful and you can freeze what's left. Dinner tonight, lunch tomorrow, and next week. Chicken and vegetables, meat, fish and seafood, beans and pulses, there's no end to the variety that soup-making offers. Smooth or chunky, clear or creamy, drinkable or forkable, soup is the answer to intimate entertaining or catering for a crowd. Enjoy some familiar flavours one day, try something more exotic another. Spend a day cooking up a big batch of stock and fill the freezer with recipe-sized portions. Then, when the desire for soup grabs you – and you know it will – it's only a saucepan and a few fresh ingredients away.

chicken stock

basic chicken stock

1.5 kg (3 lb) chicken bones
  (still with some meat on)
2 onions, halved
2 carrots, halved
2 sticks celery, chopped
8 litres (15 pints) water
8 black peppercorns
4 stalks flat-leaf parsley
2 fresh or dried bay leaves
sea salt

Preheat the oven to 200°C (400°F). Place the chicken bones, onions, carrots and celery in a large baking dish and bake for 1 hour or until well browned. Transfer to a stockpot or large saucepan with the water, peppercorns, parsley and bay leaves. Bring to the boil and allow to simmer rapidly, uncovered.

Reduce the heat so that the stock simmers slowly but constantly. Skim the surface of the stock with a spoon occasionally so that it remains clear. Simmer for 1½ hours or until the stock is well flavoured. Add a generous amount of salt to bring out the flavour.

Strain the stock through a fine sieve. Allow to cool, then remove any solidified fat from the surface. Refrigerate the stock for up to 3 days or freeze in ready-to-use portions. Makes 4 litres (7½ pints).

beef or veal stock **Replace the chicken bones in the recipe above with 1.5 kg (3 lb) of chopped brisket or good beef or veal bones (ask your butcher to chop them for you). Place in a baking dish, brush with oil, then continue as for the chicken stock.**
vegetable stock **Follow the chicken stock recipe above, but omit the chicken bones. As well as the vegetables included in the recipe, add 2 chopped leeks and 2 cups of sliced mushrooms to the stockpot with the required amount of water.**
fish stock **Replace the chicken bones in the chicken stock recipe above with the heads and bones of 3 small fish such as snapper. Do not roast the fish bones or vegetables – follow the stock recipe from step 2, adding all of the ingredients plus 1 cup (8 fl oz) of dry white wine. Simmer for 20 minutes (any longer and the stock will become sour), then strain through muslin or a very fine sieve.**

Chinese barbecue pork and egg noodle soup

roast pumpkin soup

pea and ham soup

Chinese barbecue pork and egg noodle soup

8 cups (3 1/2 pints) chicken stock
1 star anise
1 1/2 tablespoons shredded ginger
4 green onions (scallions), sliced
1 small red chilli, seeded and finely chopped
1 tablespoon Chinese cooking wine*
1 1/2 teaspoons soy sauce
250g (8 oz) gai larn*, trimmed and cut into 5 cm (2 in) lengths
300g (10 oz) fresh thin egg noodles
350g (12 oz) Chinese barbecued pork fillet*, thinly sliced

Heat the stock, star anise, ginger, green onions, chilli, cooking wine and soy sauce over medium–high heat in a large saucepan. Bring to the boil, reduce the heat and simmer for 8–10 minutes. Add the gai larn and cook for a further 1–2 minutes or until tender.
Meanwhile, place the noodles in a bowl of boiling water and allow to stand for 30 seconds. Drain.
Warm the barbecued pork.
To serve, place the noodles in bowls, pour over the soup and top with slices of pork. Serves 4.

roast pumpkin soup

2 kg (4 lb) butternut* or sweet pumpkin,
  cut into thin wedges, skin on
7 cups (3 pints) chicken or vegetable stock
1 tablespoon Dijon mustard
2 tablespoons honey
sea salt and cracked black pepper

Preheat the oven to 200°C (400°F). Place the pumpkin in a baking dish and bake for 45–55 minutes or until soft and golden.
Scrape the pumpkin from the skin. Place the flesh in a blender in two batches with 1 cup of the stock in each batch and blend until smooth. Place the pumpkin purée, remaining stock, mustard, honey, salt and pepper in a saucepan and simmer over medium heat for 5 minutes. Serve in bowls topped with flavoured sour cream (page 36) or shaved gruyère cheese. Serves 4.

pea and ham soup

1.25 kg (2 3/4 lb) smoked ham hock, chopped ▪
2.5 litres (4 1/2 pints) water
1 fresh or dried bay leaf
1 onion, roughly chopped
1 carrot, roughly chopped
1 stick celery, roughly chopped
1 1/2 cups (330g/11 1/2 oz) green split peas
sea salt and cracked black pepper
2 tablespoons chopped flat-leaf parsley

Remove the skin and fat from the pieces of hock. Place the hock in a large saucepan and pour over the water. Add the bay leaf, onion, carrot and celery then cover and simmer for 20 minutes.
Remove the hock pieces from the pan, remove the ham from the bone and chop. Strain the liquid and discard the vegetables and bay leaf.
Return the liquid and chopped ham to the pan. Add the split peas and simmer for 30–35 minutes or until soft.
To serve, stir through the salt, pepper and parsley and ladle into bowls. Serves 4–6.
▪ Ask your butcher to cut the hock into 4 pieces.

lentil, lemon and yoghurt soup

1 tablespoon olive oil
2 brown onions, finely chopped
1 teaspoon ground cumin
1 teaspoon ground coriander (cilantro)
1 1/2 cups red lentils
3 cups (1 1/2 pints) vegetable stock
4 cups (1 3/4 pints) water
1 tablespoon finely grated lemon rind
300g (10 oz) roughly chopped English spinach, optional
sea salt and cracked black pepper

Heat a large saucepan over medium–high heat. Add the oil, onion, cumin and ground coriander and cook for 6 minutes or until the onion is well browned. Add the lentils, stock, water and lemon rind and bring to the boil. Cover and allow to simmer for 15 minutes or until the lentils are soft. Stir through the English spinach, if using. To serve, stir through the salt and pepper, then ladle the soup into mugs or bowls. Combine 1 cup (8 fl oz) thick plain yoghurt and 2 tablespoons fresh coriander (cilantro) and spoon on if desired. Serves 4.

lentil, lemon and yoghurt soup

wonton soup

6 cups (2¹/₂ pints) chicken stock
2 cups (16 fl oz) water
1 tablespoon soy sauce
2 tablespoons Chinese cooking wine*
1 tablespoon shredded ginger
250g (8 oz) choy sum*, chopped
wontons
300g (10 oz) pork mince
2 green onions (scallions), chopped
2 teaspoons grated ginger
2 tablespoons hoisin sauce*
¹/₂ teaspoon sesame oil
1 teaspoon cornflour (cornstarch)
1 tablespoon water
24 wonton wrappers*

To make the wontons, combine the pork, onion, ginger, hoisin sauce and sesame oil in a bowl. Mix the cornflour and water in a small bowl. Place 1 teaspoon of the pork mixture in the centre of a wonton wrapper. Brush the edges of the wrapper with cornflour mixture, then take one corner over to the opposite corner to form a triangle. Pleat and press to enclose the filling. Repeat with the remaining wrappers and mixture. Set aside.
Place the stock, water, soy sauce, cooking wine and ginger in a large saucepan. Bring to the boil then reduce the heat and add the wontons in batches, cooking for 3 minutes or until they float to the surface.
Return all the wontons to the pan along with the choy sum and cook for 2–3 minutes or until the greens are tender. To serve, divide the wontons and greens between bowls and pour over the soup. Serves 4.

roast tomato soup

12 large vine-ripened tomatoes (2 kg/4 lb), halved
1 head garlic, whole and unpeeled
2 tablespoons olive oil
sea salt and cracked black pepper
3 cups (1¹/₂ pints) chicken stock
2–3 teaspoons sugar

Preheat the oven to 180°C (350°F). Place the tomatoes and garlic on two baking trays lined with non-stick baking paper. Drizzle with olive oil and sprinkle with salt and pepper. Bake for 40 minutes or until very soft. Allow to cool slightly. Squeeze the garlic flesh from its skin and process in a blender with the tomatoes and any juice from the baking trays in two batches until smooth.
Cook the tomato mixture, stock and sugar in a saucepan over medium heat for 6 minutes, stirring occasionally. To serve, ladle into bowls or mugs and top with a spoonful of mint pesto (page 36). Serves 4–6.

creamy spring vegetable soup

40g (1¹/₂ oz) butter
3 tablespoons plain (all-purpose) flour
2 cups (16 fl oz) milk
2 cups (16 fl oz) chicken or vegetable stock
2 cups (16 fl oz) cream
2 cups chopped broccoli florets
3 zucchini (courgettes), finely chopped
2 cups shelled fresh peas (800g/1³/₄ lb unshelled)
1 bunch (200g/7 oz) asparagus, trimmed and chopped
¹/₄ cup finely grated parmesan cheese
¹/₃ cup chopped flat-leaf parsley
sea salt and cracked black pepper

Heat the butter in a large saucepan over medium heat. Add the flour and stir for 1 minute. Remove from the heat and whisk in the milk, stock and cream. Return to the heat and stir until the mixture boils and thickens, around 3 minutes. Add the broccoli, zucchini, peas and asparagus and simmer for 5 minutes. Stir through the parmesan, parsley, salt and pepper.
Serve in deep bowls with croutons (page 36). Serves 4–6.

Thai chicken and coconut soup

2 red chillies, seeded and chopped
1 tablespoon shredded ginger
1 stalk lemongrass, bruised
6 cups (2¹/₂ pints) chicken stock
2 cups (16 fl oz) coconut cream
3 chicken breast fillets, sliced
100g (3¹/₂ oz) button mushrooms, halved
2 baby bok choy*, separated into leaves
6 kaffir lime leaves*, shredded
1 tablespoon fish sauce*
1 tablespoon lime juice

Place the chilli, ginger, lemongrass and stock in a saucepan over medium–high heat. Bring to the boil then reduce the heat, cover and simmer for 7 minutes. Remove the lemongrass, add the coconut cream and allow to simmer for another minute. Add the chicken, mushrooms, bok choy and kaffir lime leaves. Stir to separate the chicken and cook for 3 minutes or until tender. Stir through the fish sauce and lime juice and cook for a further minute.
Serve in deep bowls. Serves 4.

wonton soup

creamy spring vegetable soup

roast tomato soup

Thai chicken and coconut soup

how to bouillabaisse

3 tablespoons olive oil

1 onion, chopped

1 fennel bulb, trimmed and thinly sliced

1 leek, trimmed and sliced

1 medium red chilli, seeded and chopped

10 saffron threads

1 tablespoon boiling water

400g (14 oz) can peeled tomatoes, roughly chopped

8 cups (3½ pints) fish stock

500g (1 lb) snapper fillets, skin on, cubed

2 x 300g (10 oz) raw (green) crabs, cleaned and each cut into 6 pieces

12 medium raw (green) prawns (shrimp) (460g/15 oz), peeled, tails intact

8 scallops in half shell

2 tablespoons chopped flat-leaf parsley

Heat a large saucepan over medium–high heat. Add the oil, onion, fennel, leek and chilli and cook for 6 minutes or until soft and golden.
Meanwhile, place the saffron threads in a small heatproof bowl, pour over the boiling water and set aside for 5 minutes.

Add the tomatoes, saffron (and liquid) and stock to the pan. Bring to the boil, reduce the heat and simmer for 10 minutes.

Add the snapper, crab pieces, prawns and scallops to the broth and simmer for 2 minutes.
Stir through the parsley and serve in bowls with rouille (page 36) and croutons (page 36) if desired. Serves 4 as a main meal.

When making bouillabaisse, you can use any combination of seafood and fish, depending on what you like to eat and what is available. If you or one of your family or guests doesn't eat seafood, just use fish, or vice versa. Buy a total amount of fish or seafood approximately equivalent to the total amount of the fish and seafood combined in the recipe above.

bouillabaisse

minestrone

clam chowder

potato, bacon and leek soup

minestrone

2 teaspoons olive oil
1 onion, chopped
2 cloves garlic, sliced
1 carrot, chopped
1 kg (2 lb) smoked ham hock, chopped ▪
400g (14 oz) can peeled tomatoes
5 cups (2 pints) beef stock
1/4 cup small pasta, such as macaroni
150g (5 oz) broccoli, chopped
100g (3 1/2 oz) green beans, chopped
310g (10 oz) can cannellini beans, drained
sea salt and cracked black pepper
2 tablespoons chopped flat-leaf parsley

Cook the oil, onion, garlic and carrot in a large saucepan over medium heat for 5 minutes. Remove the skin and visible fat from the ham hock then add to the pan with the tomatoes and stock. Cover and simmer for 35 minutes. Remove the hock, cut the ham from the bone and dice. Add to the pan with the pasta, broccoli, green and cannellini beans, salt and pepper. Continue to simmer for 15 minutes. Stir through the parsley, ladle into bowls and serve with shaved parmesan cheese. Serves 4–6.
▪ Ask your butcher to cut the hock into 4 pieces.

clam chowder

25g (3/4 oz) butter
1 onion, sliced
3 rashers bacon, finely chopped
3/4 cup (6 fl oz) white wine
1 fresh or dried bay leaf
400g (14 oz) can peeled tomatoes
7 cups (3 pints) fish stock
3 potatoes, peeled and chopped into 1 cm (1/2 in) dice
1 1/2 cups (12 fl oz) water
2 kg (4 lb) fresh clams (vongole), scrubbed and cleaned
1 1/2 tablespoons chopped flat-leaf parsley
1/4 cup (2 fl oz) cream

Place the butter, onion and bacon in a large saucepan over medium heat and cook for 5–6 minutes or until soft and golden. Add the wine and cook for 1 minute. Add the bay leaf, tomatoes, stock and potato and simmer, covered, for 35 minutes or until the potato is very soft. Cool slightly. Meanwhile, heat the water in a large, deep frying pan over high heat. Add the clams, cover with a tight-fitting lid and steam for 2–3 minutes or until the shells have opened. Reserve 12 clams for serving. Remove the flesh from the remaining shells, discarding any unopened clams. Process the cooled soup in a blender in batches until smooth. Return to a clean pan, add the clam meat, parsley and cream and heat gently for 5 minutes. To serve, pour into bowls and top with the reserved clams. Serves 4.

potato, bacon and leek soup

1 tablespoon olive oil
3 leeks, trimmed and chopped
1 1/2 tablespoons finely chopped sage
6 rashers bacon, chopped
3 potatoes (825g/1 3/4 lb), peeled and chopped
7 cups (3 pints) beef stock
1/2 cup (4 fl oz) cream, optional
sea salt and cracked black pepper

Heat the oil in a large saucepan over medium heat. Add the leek and cook for 10–12 minutes or until golden. Add the sage and bacon and cook for 6 minutes or until the bacon is golden. Add the potato and stock and simmer for 15–20 minutes or until the potato is tender. Stir through the cream, if using, and add the salt and pepper. Ladle into bowls and serve with toasted bread. Serves 4.

Italian tomato and basil bread soup

2 kg (4 lb) very ripe tomatoes
2 tablespoons olive oil
2 cloves garlic, sliced
200g (7 oz) wood-fired bread
2 cups (16 fl oz) chicken or vegetable stock
1/2 cup torn basil leaves
1 teaspoon sugar
extra olive oil
cracked black pepper

To peel the tomatoes, score a cross in the skin on the base and place in a large saucepan of boiling water, leaving them there for 3 minutes. Drain, then peel. Place the oil and garlic in a large saucepan over medium heat and cook for 1 minute. Add the tomatoes and simmer for 30 minutes, stirring occasionally to break them up. Remove the crust from the bread and tear the centre into chunks. Add the bread, stock, basil and sugar to the tomatoes and allow to stand for 5 minutes. To serve, ladle the soup into bowls, drizzle with the extra olive oil and sprinkle with plenty of cracked black pepper. Serves 4–6.

Italian tomato and basil bread soup

French onion soup

how to French onion soup

8 brown onions, sliced
30g (1 oz) butter
1 tablespoon olive oil
2 tablespoons thyme leaves
2 tablespoons plain
    (all-purpose) flour
2 tablespoons brandy
2 tablespoons Dijon mustard
8 cups (3½ pints) beef stock
2 cups (16 fl oz) water

Place the onions, butter, oil and thyme in a large saucepan over medium heat, cover and cook for 35 minutes, stirring occasionally, until soft and golden.

Add the flour and cook, stirring, for 3 minutes.

Add the brandy and cook, stirring, for 1 minute. Add the mustard, stock and water and allow to simmer for 15 minutes. Ladle the soup into bowls and serve with toasted cheese sandwiches (page 36) or parmesan toasts (page 36). Serves 4–6.

The secret to making this soup is to brown the onions very well, until they are a deep golden colour, a lovely soft texture, and really sweet and flavoursome. This is quite a rich soup and is ideal served as a meal with toasted bread or sandwiches on the side. If serving as a starter, offer just a small bowl of French onion soup, or make the main course a light one.

chicken and matzo ball soup   smoky roasted gazpacho

chicken and sweet corn soup

chicken and matzo ball soup

8 cups (3 1/2 pints) chicken stock
1 large carrot, peeled and chopped
1 large celery stick, chopped
matzo balls
3 eggs, separated
1/2 cup (4 fl oz) chicken stock
3 tablespoons vegetable oil
1 tablespoon chopped flat-leaf parsley
1/2 teaspoon salt
1/2 teaspoon cracked black pepper
1 1/4 cups fine matzo meal*

To make the matzo balls, whisk together the egg yolks and stock. Add the oil, parsley, salt and pepper then gradually add the matzo meal, stirring well to combine. Whisk the eggwhites until soft peaks form then gently fold into the matzo mixture. Refrigerate for at least 6 hours until firm, then shape tablespoons of the mixture into balls.
Bring a large saucepan of water to a simmer and cook the matzo balls for 25 minutes or until cooked through.
To make the soup, place the stock, carrot and celery in a large saucepan. Bring to the boil then reduce the heat and simmer for 8 minutes or until the carrot is tender. Add the matzo balls and cook for a further 5 minutes.
To serve, ladle the matzo balls and soup into bowls. Serves 4.

smoky roasted gazpacho

4 vine-ripened tomatoes, quartered
2 cloves garlic, unpeeled
sea salt and cracked black pepper
4 red capsicums (bell peppers), quartered
1 1/2 tablespoons sherry or red wine vinegar
1/2 teaspoon smoky paprika*
1 1/2 teaspoons sugar
2 tablespoons olive oil
3 cups (1 1/2 pints) water
1 small Lebanese cucumber, finely chopped

Preheat the oven to 200°C (400°F). Place the tomatoes and garlic on a baking tray lined with non-stick baking paper. Sprinkle with salt and pepper and roast for 20–25 minutes or until soft.
Meanwhile, place the capsicums under a hot grill (broiler) skin-side up and grill (broil) until the skin is blackened. Place in a plastic bag, seal and allow to stand for 5 minutes, then remove the capsicums and peel away the skin.
Remove the skin from the tomatoes. Squeeze the garlic flesh from its skin and place in a blender with the tomatoes, capsicum, sherry or vinegar, paprika, sugar, oil and water. Blend until smooth then chill.
Ladle into mugs or bowls, sprinkle over the chopped cucumber and serve cold with crusty bread. Serves 4–6.

chicken and sweet corn soup

6 cups (2 1/2 pints) chicken stock
2 cups (16 fl oz) water
2 chicken breasts, trimmed
5 green onions (scallions), sliced
1 clove garlic, crushed
3 corn cobs (400g/14 oz), kernels removed
2 tablespoons Chinese cooking wine*
1 1/2 tablespoons soy sauce

Bring the stock and water to the boil in a large saucepan. Reduce the heat, add the chicken and simmer for 6 minutes or until cooked through.
Remove the chicken from the stock, allow to cool slightly, then shred the meat.
Add the green onions, garlic, corn kernels, cooking wine and soy sauce to the stock, simmer for 5 minutes then remove from the heat. Allow to cool slightly, then process half of the soup in a blender until smooth.
Return the processed soup to the soup in the pan, add the shredded chicken and simmer gently until heated through.
To serve, ladle into bowls and sprinkle over coriander (cilantro) leaves if desired. Serves 4.

chicken noodle soup

1.6 kg (3 1/4 lb) chicken
11 cups (4 1/2 pints) water
1 stick celery, finely chopped
1 carrot, finely chopped
1 small onion, finely chopped
1 1/2 cups macaroni or short soup noodles
2 tablespoons chopped flat-leaf parsley
sea salt and cracked black pepper

Preheat the oven to 200°C (400°F). Place the chicken on a greased rack in a baking dish, prick the skin all over and bake for 1 hour or until golden brown.
Bring the water to the boil in a large saucepan over high heat with the lid on. Transfer the whole cooked chicken to the saucepan and add the celery, carrot and onion. Cover and cook for 15 minutes.
Remove the chicken from the pan and allow to cool slightly. Remove and discard the skin, then remove the meat from the bones and chop. Skim any fat from the top of the stock, then strain the liquid and return to the pan. Place the chopped chicken meat and macaroni in the pan and cook for 12 minutes or until the pasta is soft.
Stir through the parsley, pepper and plenty of salt, ladle into bowls and serve with toasted bread. Serves 4.

chicken noodle soup

how to laksa

800g (1 3/4 lb) medium raw (green) prawns (shrimp)
5 cups (2 pints) water
2–3 tablespoons laksa paste ■
3 cups (1 1/2 pints) coconut milk
3 teaspoons fish sauce*
150g (5 oz) snow peas (mange tout), trimmed and halved
4 kaffir lime leaves*, shredded
250g (8 oz) dry rice vermicelli noodles
1 cup beansprouts
1/4 cup Vietnamese mint* or regular mint leaves
1/4 cup coriander (cilantro) leaves
1 large red chilli, sliced

Peel the prawns, reserving the shells and heads. To make the prawn stock, place the shells and heads in a large frying pan and cook over high heat for 7 minutes or until the shells are golden and cooked. Add the water and simmer for 5 minutes, then remove from the heat and strain through a fine sieve.

Place the laksa paste in a saucepan over medium heat and cook, stirring, for 3 minutes. Add the prawn stock, coconut milk and fish sauce and simmer for 5 minutes, then add the prawns, snow peas and kaffir lime leaves. Cook for a further 3 minutes or until the prawns have changed colour and are tender.

Place the noodles in a bowl of boiling water and allow to stand for 2 minutes or until soft. Drain. To serve, place the noodles, beansprouts, mint and coriander in bowls. Spoon over the laksa liquid, prawns and snow peas and top with the chilli. Serve with lime wedges. Serves 4.

There are a few versions of this spicy soup that originated in Singapore, known there as laksa lemak and now so popular elsewhere it has modern classic status. Shrimp paste and chillies are two of the important ingredients that give laksa paste its distinctive flavour. In Singapore, Vietnamese mint* is known as laksa leaf.
■ The heat of different laksa pastes will vary. For the best flavour, buy a good-quality laksa paste, or make your own (see glossary).

laksa

short order

croutons

rouille

bruschetta

short order

croutons

Slice half a loaf white unsliced bread into 2 cm (3/4 in) cubes. Toss in a bowl with 2 teaspoons thyme leaves, 1 tablespoon olive oil, sea salt and cracked black pepper. Place on a baking tray lined with non-stick baking paper and bake for 15 minutes at 180°C (350°F) or until golden. Sprinkle over soup just before serving.

rouille

Grill (broil) 2 red capsicums (bell peppers) skin-side up under a hot grill (broiler) until blackened. Place in a plastic bag, seal, allow to cool, then remove skin. Process the capsicum flesh, 1 medium seeded red chilli and 2 cloves garlic in a food processor until smooth. With the motor running, slowly add 2 tablespoons olive oil, then stir through 1/4 cup fresh white breadcrumbs. Serve with bouillabaisse. Makes approximately 1 cup.

bruschetta

Place 8 slices crusty Italian-style bread under a hot grill (broiler) and cook until golden. Brush with olive oil then rub with the cut side of a garlic clove. Sprinkle with sea salt and cracked black pepper and serve with any robust soup.

rough pesto

Roughly chop 1 cup basil leaves and mix with 1 clove crushed garlic, 1/3 cup finely grated parmesan cheese, 1/4 cup toasted and roughly chopped pine nuts and 1/3 cup (2 1/2 fl oz) olive oil. Serve spoonfuls on top of vegetable and big, hearty soups.

mint pesto

Roughly chop 1 cup mint leaves, 1/2 cup flat-leaf parsley, 1/4 cup toasted pine nuts and 1/4 cup finely grated parmesan cheese in a blender or food processor. Add 1/4 cup (2 fl oz) olive oil and blend until combined. Serve spoonfuls on top of tomato, lentil or vegetable soups.

toasted cheese sandwiches

Combine 1 1/3 cups grated cheddar cheese, 1/3 cup (2 1/2 fl oz) sour cream, 2 1/2 teaspoons Dijon mustard, sea salt and cracked black pepper in a bowl and mix well. Spread onto 4 slices bread, top with 4 more slices then spread a little butter over the outside of the sandwiches. Cook in a non-stick frying pan over medium–high heat for 1 minute on each side, pressing down firmly, until golden and crisp.

parmesan toasts

Top 4 slices crusty bread with 1 cup roughly grated parmesan cheese. Cook under a hot grill (broiler) until golden. Serve with any soup that is complemented by the flavour of parmesan.

flavoured sour cream

Combine 1 cup (8 fl oz) sour cream, 3 tablespoons chopped chives and cracked black pepper. Great with pumpkin and vegetable soups.

rough pesto

mint pesto

toasted cheese sandwiches

parmesan toasts

flavoured sour cream

salads

fresh
crisp
fast

Give me a big plate of salad any day. Especially those days when nothing but *fresh, clean flavours* will *make me happy.* Salad days. Sometimes I like to toss together a simple leaf and tomato salad as a side dish and liven it up with a dressing with a difference. Other times I'll create a main meal masterpiece that features chicken or seafood or meat, something that spells substance and stamina and satisfaction.

The salad is one of those meals a busy person can always rely on. I do. It's fast, easy and a great way to keep up the fresh vegie intake. A salad can also give you an *instant lift* somehow, with its crisp and invigorating character and flavours. And it can balance or complete a meal that has rich or fried or fatty ingredients. *On its own or as something on the side*

I'd use just one word to describe a classic salad – brilliant.

mayonnaise

basic mayonnaise

1 egg
1 tablespoon lemon juice
2 teaspoons Dijon mustard
sea salt and ground white pepper
1 cup (8 fl oz) vegetable oil

Process or blend the egg, lemon juice, mustard, salt and pepper in a food processor or blender until well combined.

With the motor running, pour the oil in very slowly in a thin stream and process until the mixture is thick and creamy.

Makes 1¼ cups.

for tartare **Stir through 1 tablespoon rinsed and chopped salted capers*, 2 tablespoons chopped cornichons or gherkins, 1 tablespoon chopped dill and 1 teaspoon lemon juice.**

for aioli **Drizzle 1 head garlic with a little olive oil, wrap in foil and bake in a preheated 180°C (350°F) oven for 30 minutes. Cool then squeeze flesh from skin. Add sea salt, mix to a paste then fold through basic mayonnaise.**

for lemon and herb mayonnaise **Stir through 2 teaspoons lemon juice and 2 teaspoons each chopped dill, parsley and basil.**

tomato and bocconcini salad

tabouli

coleslaw

tomato and bocconcini salad

3 vine-ripened tomatoes, sliced
3–4 bocconcini*, sliced
1/3 cup baby basil leaves
1/4 cup (2 fl oz) fruity extra-virgin olive oil
1 1/2 tablespoons balsamic vinegar
sea salt and cracked black pepper

Arrange the tomato, bocconcini and basil on a large plate.
Combine the oil with the vinegar, drizzle over the salad
and sprinkle with salt and pepper.
Serve with crusty bread. Serves 4 as a side dish or as
a simple starter.

tabouli

1/2 cup fine cracked wheat (burghul)*
3/4 cup (6 fl oz) water
1 1/3 cups chopped flat-leaf parsley
1 cup chopped mint
2 tomatoes, chopped
3 green onions (scallions), sliced
2 tablespoons olive oil
1 1/2 tablespoons lemon juice
sea salt and cracked black pepper

Place the wheat in a bowl and pour over the water.
Allow to stand for 20 minutes or until the water is
completely absorbed.
Place the wheat, parsley, mint, tomato, onions, oil, lemon
juice, salt and pepper in a bowl and toss to combine.
Serve as a salad or side dish with pita bread and hummus
(page 60) or grilled lamb. Serves 4 as a side dish.

coleslaw

1/2 cabbage (2 kg/4 lb)
4 green onions (scallions), thinly sliced
1/4 cup flat-leaf parsley leaves
8 radishes, thinly sliced
cracked black pepper
dressing
1 egg
1 tablespoon white wine vinegar
2 teaspoons salted capers*, rinsed
1/3 cup (2 1/2 fl oz) vegetable oil

To make the dressing, process the egg, vinegar and
capers in a food processor until combined. With the
motor running, gradually pour in the vegetable oil.
Slice the cabbage into thin wedges and place on
serving plates. Spoon over the dressing and top with
the onions, parsley, radishes and cracked black pepper.
Serves 4–6 as a side dish.

potato salad

1 kg (2 lb) waxy potatoes such as kipfler or new
1/4 cup chopped flat-leaf parsley
3 green onions (scallions), chopped
dressing
1/2 cup (4 fl oz) good-quality egg mayonnaise ■
1/2 cup (4 fl oz) sour cream
sea salt and cracked black pepper

Place the potatoes in a saucepan of boiling water and
cook for 7–10 minutes or until soft. Drain. Refrigerate
until cool, then cut in half.
To make the dressing, combine the mayonnaise, sour
cream, salt and pepper.
Toss the potatoes with the parsley, onion and dressing and
chill until ready to serve. Serves 4 as a side dish.
■ You can use the mayonnaise recipe on page 43.

potato salad

caesar salad

how to caesar salad

6 rashers bacon
1 large cos (romaine) lettuce
sea salt and cracked black pepper
¼ cup shaved parmesan cheese
croutons
1 thin baguette, sliced (32 slices)
olive oil
1 clove garlic, halved
dressing
1 egg yolk
2 teaspoons Dijon mustard
1 clove garlic, chopped
2 tablespoons lemon juice
3 anchovy fillets
¼ cup finely grated parmesan cheese
½ cup (4 fl oz) vegetable oil   .

To make the croutons, preheat the oven to 180°C (350°F). Place the baguette slices on a baking tray, brush with the olive oil and bake for 10 minutes or until crisp and golden. Rub each slice with the cut garlic and set aside.

Place the bacon on a baking tray and cook under a hot grill (broiler) until crisp. When cooled, tear into large pieces. Trim the lettuce leaves, reserving the smaller inner leaves and roughly chopping the larger ones.

To make the dressing, process the egg yolk, mustard, garlic, lemon juice, anchovies and parmesan in a food processor until combined. With the motor running, gradually add the oil and process until smooth and creamy.
To serve, toss together the lettuce, two-thirds of the dressing, the bacon, croutons, salt and pepper. Spoon over the remaining dressing and top with the shaved parmesan. Serves 4.

pear, rocket and blue cheese salad

Vietnamese noodle salad   Greek salad

pear, rocket and blue cheese salad

4 slices crusty Italian bread
150g (5 oz) rocket (arugula) leaves
2 baby fennel, thinly sliced
2 pears, thinly sliced
200g (7 oz) blue cheese
balsamic vinegar
extra-virgin olive oil
sea salt and cracked black pepper

Grill or toast the bread until crisp. Arrange on plates with
the rocket, fennel, pears and wedges of blue cheese. To
serve, drizzle over a little vinegar and oil, and sprinkle with
salt and pepper. Serves 4 as a starter or side dish.

Vietnamese noodle salad

4 teaspoons peanut oil
2 chicken breasts, diced
500g (1 lb) raw (green) prawns (shrimp),
    peeled and halved lengthwise
125g (4 oz) bean thread noodles*
1 large carrot, cut into thin strips
3 green onions (scallions), sliced
1/4 cup Vietnamese mint*, shredded
1/2 cup coriander (cilantro) leaves
dressing
1/4 cup (2 fl oz) lime juice
2 tablespoons fish sauce*
1 tablespoon brown sugar

Heat a large frying pan or wok over high heat. Add half
of the oil and stir-fry the chicken for 5–6 minutes until
cooked through and golden. Transfer to a large bowl.
Add the remaining oil to the pan and cook the prawns for
3–4 minutes or until cooked through and pink. Transfer to
the bowl with the chicken.
To make the dressing, combine the lime juice, fish sauce
and sugar, stirring until the sugar is dissolved.
Place the noodles in a heatproof bowl, cover with boiling
water and set aside for 4 minutes or until tender. Drain.
Combine the chicken, prawns, dressing, noodles, carrot,
onions, mint and coriander. To serve, sprinkle with
2 tablespoons of chopped unsalted peanuts if desired.
Serves 4.

Greek salad

4 vine-ripened tomatoes, quartered
2 Lebanese cucumbers, sliced thickly
    lengthwise and halved
1 cup flat-leaf parsley leaves
1/4 cup mint leaves, halved lengthwise
1 cup kalamata or firm black olives
250g (8 oz) fetta cheese, sliced
cracked black pepper
dressing
2 tablespoons olive oil
1 tablespoon red wine vinegar
sea salt and cracked black pepper

To make the dressing, whisk together the oil, vinegar, salt
and pepper.
Place the tomatoes, cucumbers, parsley, mint and olives
in a serving bowl. Pour over the dressing and top with the
fetta and cracked black pepper. Serve with lemon wedges
if desired. Serves 4–6 as a side dish.

niçoise salad

12 baby new potatoes, halved
300g (10 oz) green beans, halved
400g (14 oz) tuna steaks
olive oil for brushing
150g (5 oz) baby spinach or lettuce leaves
2 tomatoes, sliced
2/3 cup black olives
2 hard-boiled eggs, quartered, optional
dressing
1/3 cup (2 1/2 fl oz) olive oil
2 tablespoons red wine or sherry vinegar
2 teaspoons Dijon mustard
1 tablespoon chopped flat-leaf parsley
sea salt and cracked black pepper

Place the potatoes in a saucepan of boiling water and
cook for 5 minutes or until almost soft. Add the beans
and cook for 2 minutes or until the beans and potatoes
are tender. Drain and cool under running water.
Brush the tuna with a little olive oil. Barbecue, char-grill
(broil) or pan-fry for 1 minute each side or until the tuna
is seared but not cooked all the way through. Set aside for
5 minutes then slice.
To make the dressing, place the oil, vinegar, mustard,
parsley, salt and pepper in a bowl and whisk to combine.
Place the spinach or lettuce, tomatoes, olives, potatoes,
beans, tuna and dressing in a bowl and toss lightly.
Add eggs, if using, and serve immediately. Serves 4.

niçoise salad

how to Thai beef salad

650g (21 oz) rump, fillet or sirloin steak, trimmed
oil for brushing
150g (5 oz) salad greens
2 small red onions, finely sliced
10 kaffir lime leaves*, shredded
3 large mild chillies, seeded and shredded
2/3 cup coriander (cilantro) leaves
2/3 cup mint leaves
2/3 cup basil leaves
dressing
1 teaspoon soy sauce
2 tablespoons fish sauce*
2 tablespoons lime juice
2 tablespoons brown or palm sugar

Brush the beef with a little oil and char-grill (broil), barbecue or pan-fry until cooked to your liking (medium rare is best for this salad). Set aside for 5 minutes then slice thinly.

Place the salad greens, onions, kaffir lime leaves, chilli, coriander, mint and basil in a bowl and toss lightly.

To make the dressing, combine the soy sauce, fish sauce, lime juice and sugar. Place the beef on the salad and pour over the dressing. Serve immediately. Serves 4.

substitutes **Use this recipe as the basis for other Thai-style salads. Simply substitute the beef with the same amount of pork fillets, chicken breasts or thigh fillets, or some firm tofu. The other salad and dressing ingredients are unchanged.**
assemble later **When preparing this salad in advance, cook the beef, prepare the salad and make the dressing but store each in separate containers. Do not combine until you are ready to serve. This is an ideal portable lunch or picnic dish that can be transported in three small containers and assembled on the spot.**

Thai beef salad

octopus salad

chicken spaghetti salad

octopus salad

1.5 kg (3 lb) baby octopus
1/2 cup (4 fl oz) olive oil
1/2 cup (4 fl oz) lemon juice
2 tablespoons shredded lemon zest
1/3 cup thyme sprigs
2 tablespoons sugar
sea salt and cracked black pepper
200g (7 oz) curly endive (frisée)
1 red onion, sliced
olive oil, extra

Wash the octopus, remove the heads and beaks and
discard. Cut in half and place in a bowl with the oil,
lemon juice and zest, thyme, sugar, salt and pepper.
Cover and refrigerate for at least 3 hours.
To cook, preheat a barbecue or grill (broiler) over
high heat. Cook the octopus for 1–2 minutes each side
or until tender.
Place the curly endive and onion on plates. Top with the
octopus, drizzle with the extra oil and sprinkle with sea
salt. Serve with lemon wedges. Serves 4.

chicken spaghetti salad

400g (14 oz) spaghetti
2 teaspoons olive oil
3 chicken breast fillets
100g (3 1/2 oz) baby spinach leaves, roughly shredded
250g (8 oz) cherry tomatoes, quartered
sea salt and cracked black pepper
dressing
2 eggs
2 tablespoons Dijon mustard
4 tablespoons lemon juice
sea salt and cracked black pepper
2/3 cup (5 fl oz) vegetable oil
1/2 cup chopped basil

Cook the pasta in a large saucepan of boiling water until
al dente. Drain.
Heat a large frying pan over medium heat, add the oil
and chicken and cook until golden and cooked through.
Cool slightly then shred.
To make the dressing, process the eggs, mustard, lemon
juice, salt and pepper in a food processor or blender.
With the motor running, slowly pour in the vegetable oil.
Stir through the basil.
Combine the chicken with the spinach leaves, tomatoes,
salt, pepper and pasta. Toss through the dressing and
serve with crusty bread. Serves 4.

short order

Asian dressing

parmesan oil

hummus

short order

Asian dressing

Whisk together 1/4 cup (2 fl oz) lime juice, 1 tablespoon brown sugar, 3 teaspoons fish sauce*, 1 teaspoon soy sauce, 1 1/2 tablespoons water, 1 seeded and finely chopped red chilli and 1 1/2 teaspoons finely chopped coriander (cilantro) leaves until well combined and the sugar is dissolved. Serve over noodle salads and vegetables. Makes 1/2 cup.

parmesan oil

Cook 1 cup good-quality extra-virgin olive oil with 100g (3 1/2 oz) thickly sliced parmesan cheese in a small saucepan over very low heat without stirring for 10 minutes. Remove from the heat, add 1/2 teaspoon black peppercorns and set aside for at least 2 hours to allow the flavours to infuse. Mix the oil with a squeeze of lemon juice or a dash of vinegar and serve over a tomato and leaf salad. Makes 1 cup.

hummus

Process 400g (14 oz) drained canned chickpeas, 3 tablespoons tahini, 3 tablespoons lemon juice, 1/4 cup (2 fl oz) water, 1/2 teaspoon cumin, 1 clove crushed garlic, sea salt and cracked black pepper in a food processor until combined. With the motor running, gradually pour in 2 tablespoons olive oil, processing until just smooth. Serve with tabouli. Makes 1 3/4 cups.

avocado salsa

Combine 2 diced ripe avocados, 1/2 diced red onion, 1/4 cup coriander (cilantro) leaves and 1 seeded and shredded red chilli. Mix together 1 tablespoon olive oil, 1 1/2 tablespoons lemon or lime juice, sea salt and cracked black pepper. Pour dressing over avocado salsa and stir carefully to combine. Serve as a side dish to a salad or grilled meat or fish.

tomato and basil salsa

Combine 4 diced vine-ripened tomatoes, 2 tablespoons rinsed and drained salted capers, 1/4 cup sliced black olives and 1/2 cup small basil leaves. Mix together 1 tablespoon olive oil, 1 teaspoon sugar, sea salt and cracked black pepper and stir until the sugar is dissolved. Pour over the salsa and serve with grilled meat or fish or on toasted bread.

basic vinaigrette

Whisk together 1/3 cup (2 1/2 fl oz) good-quality extra-virgin olive oil, 2 tablespoons white wine vinegar, 1 teaspoon Dijon mustard, 1 teaspoon finely chopped flat-leaf parsley, sea salt and cracked black pepper until well combined. Serve over any leaf salad. Makes 1/2 cup.

balsamic dressing

Whisk together 1/3 cup (2 1/2 fl oz) good-quality extra-virgin olive oil, 1 1/2 tablespoons balsamic vinegar, 2 teaspoons lime juice, 1 1/2 teaspoons brown sugar, sea salt and cracked black pepper until well combined. Serve over a leaf, tomato or vegetable salad. Makes 1/2 cup.

buttermilk (ranch) dressing

Combine 3 tablespoons buttermilk, 1/4 cup (2 fl oz) sour cream, 2 teaspoons white wine vinegar and 1 teaspoon Dijon mustard. Stir through 2 teaspoons chopped chives, 1 1/2 teaspoons finely chopped parsley, sea salt and cracked black pepper. Serve over a leaf salad. Or stir through 75g (2 1/2 oz) crumbled blue vein cheese for a creamy blue cheese dressing to serve with a leaf or pear and parmesan salad. Makes 2/3 cup.

avocado salsa

tomato and basil salsa

basic vinaigrette

balsamic dressing

buttermilk (ranch) dressing

BUSH TUCKER | Making most of local produce

Going wild over gourmet delights

SPECIAL: Marion Chambers with platters of wild food.   Picture: MARK BRAKE

NIGEL AUSTIN

EXPERIENCING the life, culture and food of different countries has helped in the creation of Marion Chambers' exciting "wild food" cuisine on Kangaroo Island.

She specialises in making exotic products from rare and unusual native plants.

Ms Chambers runs the Penguin Stop Cafe and Wilderness Gourmet Catering, focusing on "wild food" and local produce at Middle Terrace, Penneshaw.

"Wilderness Gourmet Catering just grew out of producing something fine and special," she said.

"The food is seasonally adjusted and we cater for functions such as barbecues in the bush, picnics on the beach and weddings.

"It's a small, very diverse community and we try to meet the demand."

The main part of the business is the cafe, providing lunches and dinners in the high season.

Exotic local products such as samphire, wild garlic, boxthorn berry jams and chutneys, muntries, native cranberries and warragul spinach are all on the menu when in season.

Ms Chambers has sent sam-

KANGAROO ISLAND

phire – a native plant comparable to a miniature asparagus – to Neil Perry's famous Rockpool restaurant in Sydney and to Bethany Finn at Urban Bistro in Adelaide.

The samphire is also sold in the Penguin Stop Cafe during season. Ms Chambers also makes pesto from it and wild garlic.

The garlic comes from stands that have survived on the island since it was introduced by passengers on early ships to the region.

Ms Chambers admits finding pickers is sometimes the hardest part of her job. She often uses backpackers and local enthusiasts.

The range includes berry syrup, made from boxthorns originally brought to the island for wind protection.

There also are muntries from local groundcover bushes that are used in chutneys and muffins.

"I often do food platters and these things generate lots of interest," she said.

Ms Chambers is very excited about the potential for delicious homegrown premium Kangaroo Island lamb and beef, which she has just starting marketing through the cafe outlet.

allow men believe in
. Strong men believe
cause and effect."

Ralph Waldo Emerson

Ralph could write the words that so eloquently describe the benefits of punting with the TAB.

low thinkers may well bundle TAB punting in with other "games of chance".

look deeper realise that the TAB offers more rewards than pure luck could ever deliver.

wn knowledge by studying the form guide or by simply using the ratings. The effect might not

ning selection. But at least you'll have the satisfaction of knowing what caused the result.

www.TABonline.com.au

Korp cremation row

A ROW has erupted over funeral arrangements for Maria Korp.

Mrs Korp's daughter Laura De Gois has decided to have her mother cremated but the family of her husband Joe says this was against her wishes.

The solicitor for Ms De Gois, Jim Robinson, said the law stated decisions on disposition of a body were taken by the executor, in this case Ms De Gois.

He said cremation had been chosen after consultation with Mrs Korp's Catholic priest.

But Joe Korp's brother Gust said his sister-in-law had feared cremation.

bargainbuys

SUPERMARKETS

WOOLWORTHS	Bargain Price	Normal Price	BI-LO	Bargain Price	Normal Price
Chicken Breast Fillets Skin off (kg)	8.88	13.99	Smiths Potato Chips (200g)	1.59	-
John West Tuna Plain/Flavoured (100g)	1.00	1.62	Skinless Chicken Breast Fillet (Min. 1.2kg for)	8.47	11.99
COLES			**IGA**		
Flora Spread (500g)	1.49	2.60	Kirks/Deep Spring (1.25 litre)	.89	1.51
Kleenex Cottonelle Toilet Tissue (8 Pk)	4.99	5.49	Radiant Laundry (1kg/1.5 litre)	3.79	6.05
FOODLAND IGA					
SPC Fruit (825g)	1.59	2.64			
Spree Conc. Liquid or Cuddly (1kg/1 litre)	1.69	2.59			

FISHMARKETS

SAMTASS			ANGELAKIS BROS		
Raw Prawn Meat Imp. 1kg Bags (each)	15.99	-	Fresh Black Mussels (kg)	5.90	-
Large Prawn Meat Imp. Cooked/Peeled (kg)	17.99	-	Fresh Leatherjackets (kg)	6.90	-
INTERNATIONAL OYSTER & SEAFOODS			**CAPPO SEAFOODS**		
Seafood Ravioli 500g Pk (each)	8.20	-	Fresh Whole Mulloway (kg)	5.99	-
Fresh Swordfish Steaks (kg)	22.90	-	Fresh Atlantic Salmon Steaks (kg)	26.90	-
RAPTIS FISH MARKETS			**NEW WAVE SEAFOODS**		
Queen Snapper (kg)	2.99	-	Green Prawn Meat Medium (Min. 300g for)	12.90	-
Half-Shell Scallops (dozen)	6.99	-	Smoked Salmon Sliced (Min. 1kg) (kg)	28.50	-

Time to clean up with savings

YOU can clean up this week with big savings on laundry detergent.

At Foodland, you can pick up 825g SPC Fruit for $1.59 and Spree and Cuddly laundry detergent for $1.69.

Radiant laundry powder costs just $3.79 at IGA.

The store also is of-

will cost $12.90 for 300g and smoked sliced salmon only $28.50/kg with a minimum purchase of 1kg at New Wave Australia.

At Angelakis Bros fresh black mussels are out for $5.90/kg and fresh leatherjackets a $6.90/kg.

Samtass Bros are of

vegetables

*versatile
seasonal
bountiful*

The potato, the pea, the eggplant, the zucchini. Corn, pumpkin, spinach and capsicum. All capable of *such great things* in the right hands in the kitchen. Equip yourself with a good selection of whatever vegetables are in season, and you'll never be stuck for an entree, main meal, snack or side dish ever again.

The secret is to *use vegetables as inspired ingredients*, not something you have to serve for the sake of colour and good health – even though they rate highly on both. Make the most of the creamy *simplicity* of mashed potato, the *completeness* of roast vegetable lasagne, the freshness of vegetable rice paper rolls, the *anticipation* as the pumpkin and goat's cheese pizza bakes in the oven and fills the house with its irresistible aroma.

I really like cooking for my *vegetable-loving friends.* They praise dishes like the roast vegetable frittata as a work of art, the spinach and cheddar soufflé as heavenly. And so they should.

mash

basic mash

7 good mashing potatoes (1.5 kg/3 lb) such as Desiree,
Sebago, Spunta, Idaho or Russet Burbanks
85g (2^1/$_2$ oz) butter
^{1}/$_2$–^{3}/$_4$ cup (4–6 fl oz) milk, warmed
sea salt

Peel and chop the potatoes. Place in a saucepan of boiling water.

Cook the potatoes over medium–high heat until soft. Drain.

Return to the warm pan and add the butter and ^{1}/$_2$ cup (4 fl oz) of the milk. Mash and add salt. You may need to add the extra milk depending on the type of potato. Serves 4–6 as a side dish.

mustard mash **Add ^{1}/$_3$ cup Dijon mustard with the butter and milk in step 3 of the basic mash recipe above. Great served with roast meats or chicken.**
minted pea mash **Cook 2 cups peas (fresh or frozen) in boiling water for 5 minutes. Drain. Place with a few spoonfuls of the basic mash in a food processor and pulse until roughly chopped. Add the pea mixture to the remaining mash in the pan and mix until combined. Add chopped mint and sea salt to taste. Great with grilled lamb. Serves 4–6 as a side dish.**
potato and celeriac mash **Cook 5 Desiree potatoes (900g/1^3/$_4$ lb) and 600g (20 oz) peeled and chopped celeriac (1 kg/2 lb whole) in a saucepan of boiling water until soft. Drain and return to the warm pan. Add 85g (2^1/$_2$ oz) butter and ^{1}/$_3$–^{1}/$_2$ cup (2^1/$_2$–4 fl oz) warmed milk. Mash and add sea salt to taste. Serves 4–6 as a side dish.**

vegetable tempura

potato rösti

vegetable stir-fry

vegetable tempura

1 eggplant (aubergine), sliced lengthwise
1 bunch (150g/5 oz) asparagus, trimmed
500g (1 lb) jap pumpkin*, sliced
350g (11½ oz) white sweet potato*, sliced
12 green beans, trimmed
peanut oil for deep-frying
batter
2 cups plain (all-purpose) flour
2 cups (16 fl oz) chilled soda water
dipping sauce
¼ cup (2 fl oz) mirin*
2 tablespoons soy sauce
2 tablespoons water
1 teaspoon grated ginger

To make the dipping sauce, cook the mirin, soy sauce, water and ginger in a small saucepan over medium heat for 3–4 minutes. Set aside and keep warm.
To make the batter (it is important to do this just before cooking), place the flour in a bowl and pour over the cold soda water. Stir to just combine; the batter should be quite lumpy, not smooth.
Heat the oil in a large saucepan to medium–high. Dip the vegetables into the batter a few at a time, coating them well. Fry the battered vegetables in batches for 2–3 minutes or until tender and very light golden. Keep warm in a low oven while cooking the remaining vegetables. Serve immediately with the dipping sauce. Serves 6.

potato rösti

4 roasting potatoes (850g/1¾ lb) such as
    Desiree, Pontiac and Sebago, peeled
1½ tablespoons olive oil
⅓ cup finely grated parmesan cheese
1½ teaspoons thyme leaves
sea salt and cracked black pepper

Preheat the oven to 200°C (400°F). Using a sharp vegetable peeler, cut the potato into long, thin strips. Toss the potato strips with the oil, parmesan, thyme, salt and pepper. Place the mixture in six piles on a baking tray lined with non-stick baking paper. Bake for 20–25 minutes or until golden and cooked through. Serve with meats or fish. Serves 4–6 as a side dish.

vegetable stir-fry

1 tablespoon peanut oil
2 large red chillies, seeded and sliced
2 onions, sliced into thin wedges
2 cloves garlic, sliced
¼ teaspoon cracked black pepper
200g (7 oz) green beans, trimmed
1 red capsicum (bell pepper), sliced
2 zucchini (courgettes), sliced
2 cups broccoli florets
200g (7 oz) snow peas (mange tout), trimmed
2 tablespoons soy sauce
1 tablespoon sugar
2 tablespoons small basil leaves
¼ cup roasted unsalted cashews

Heat a wok or large frying pan over high heat. Cook the oil, chillies, onions, garlic and pepper for 2 minutes. Add the beans, capsicum, zucchini, broccoli and snow peas and stir-fry for 4–5 minutes or until tender. Toss through the soy sauce and sugar. Sprinkle with the basil and cashews and serve with jasmine rice or as a side dish. Serves 4 as a side dish or with rice as a meal.

potato chips

4 large, long potatoes (1.3 kg/2¾ lb) such as Spunta,
    Russet Burbanks, King Edward
peanut oil
sea salt

To cook the chips in the oven, preheat to 220°C (425°F). Scrub the potatoes and cut into long, thin chips. Place in a bowl and toss with a little oil. Place two baking trays in the oven and allow to heat for 15 minutes. Cut pieces of non-stick baking paper to fit the trays. Keeping the trays as hot as possible, place the baking paper on the trays then sprinkle the potatoes over. Bake for 20 minutes then turn the chips using tongs. Bake for a further 10 minutes or until crisp. Sprinkle generously with salt and serve immediately.
To fry the chips, scrub the potatoes and cut into long, thin chips. Heat enough oil for deep-frying in a saucepan over medium heat; the oil should be at 160°C (325°F). Fry the potato chips in small batches for 3 minutes then place on a tray. When all of the chips are fried, fry them again for 3 minutes so that they are golden and extra crisp. Drain on paper towel and sprinkle with salt. Serve immediately. Serves 4.

potato chips

roast vegetable frittata

how to roast vegetable frittata

600g (20 oz) orange sweet potato* or pumpkin, peeled and chopped
1 red capsicum (bell pepper), cut into eight pieces
2 zucchini (courgettes), quartered
4 baby new potatoes, quartered
olive oil and sea salt for sprinkling
frittata mix
6 eggs
1 cup (8 fl oz) cream
$1/2$ cup grated aged cheddar or parmesan cheese
2 tablespoons shredded basil
cracked black pepper

Preheat the oven to 180°C (350°F). Place the sweet potato or pumpkin, capsicum, zucchini and potatoes on a baking tray lined with non-stick baking paper. Drizzle with oil and sprinkle with salt. Bake for 40 minutes or until soft and golden.

Place the vegetables in a 20 cm (8 in) non-stick frying pan. To make the frittata, whisk together the eggs, cream, cheese, basil and pepper. Pour over the vegetables in the frying pan and cook over low heat for 8–10 minutes or until the frittata begins to set.

Place the frittata under a preheated hot grill (broiler) and cook for 2 minutes or until golden. Allow to stand for 5 minutes before slicing into thick wedges. Serve immediately with a simple salad or toast. Serves 4–6.

Other combinations of cooked vegetables can be used to make frittata – char-grilled eggplant (aubergine) and mushrooms work really well. You can also use leftover roast vegetables and add ingredients such as chopped cooked chicken, drained canned tuna, other kinds of hard cheeses and fresh herbs.

potato, pea and spinach curry   roast vegetable lasagne

74

potato, pea and spinach curry

1 tablespoon peanut oil
1 teaspoon black mustard seeds*
1 onion, chopped
2 cloves garlic, finely chopped
1 teaspoon ground cumin
1 teaspoon ground coriander (cilantro)
4 waxy potatoes (800g/13/4 lb), peeled and chopped
440g (14 oz) can peeled tomatoes, lightly crushed
11/4 cups fresh peas (500g/1 lb in their pods)
6 fresh or dry curry leaves*
1 teaspoon garam masala
1 bunch (400g/14 oz) English spinach, trimmed

Heat the oil in a deep frying pan over medium heat.
Add the mustard seeds, cover and cook until they pop.
Add the onion, garlic, cumin, coriander and cook,
uncovered, for 1 minute. Add the potato and tomato and
cook for 7 minutes, stirring occasionally. Add the peas,
curry leaves, garam masala and spinach. Cook, stirring
occasionally, for 5 minutes or until the potato is soft. Serve
with steamed rice and cucumber and yoghurt (page 86).
Serves 4 as a meal or 6 as a side dish.

roast vegetable lasagne

8 vine-ripened tomatoes, thickly sliced
3 orange sweet potatoes*, peeled and thinly sliced
2 eggplants (aubergines), thickly sliced
3 red capsicums (bell peppers), cut into eight pieces
5 zucchini (courgettes), thickly sliced lengthwise
4 field mushrooms, sliced
sea salt for sprinkling
375g (121/2 oz) fresh lasagne sheets ■
ricotta filling
1 kg (2 lb) fresh ricotta
1/4 cup chopped basil leaves
1/4 cup chopped flat-leaf parsley leaves
2 eggs
3/4 cup (6 fl oz) cream
sea salt and cracked black pepper
1 cup grated mozzarella

Preheat the oven to 180°C (350°F). Place the tomatoes,
sweet potatoes, eggplants, capsicums, zucchini and
mushrooms on baking trays lined with non-stick baking
paper. Sprinkle with salt and bake for 40 minutes or until
tender and golden.
To make the ricotta filling, combine the ricotta, basil,
parsley, eggs, cream, salt and pepper.
Grease a 32 cm (123/4 in) x 22 cm (9 in) or similar
ovenproof baking dish. Line with some of the lasagne
sheets. Place half of the vegetables on top, then another
lasagne sheet. Spoon over half of the ricotta mixture, then
place another layer of lasagne sheets on top. Continue
layering, finishing with the ricotta mixture.
Sprinkle with the mozzarella and bake for 45 minutes or
until the vegetables are soft. Serves 6–8.
■ You can also use dry lasagne sheets that have been
cooked in boiling water until soft.

peas with pancetta and mint

vegetable rice paper rolls

pumpkin and goat's cheese pizza

peas with pancetta and mint

1/4 cup (2 fl oz) chicken stock
2 1/2 cups fresh peas (1 kg/2 lb in the pod)
6 slices pancetta
30g (1 oz) butter
1 tablespoon shredded mint leaves
cracked black pepper

Bring the stock to the boil in a saucepan over
medium–high heat. Add the peas, cover and cook for
5 minutes or until tender.
While the peas are cooking, cook the pancetta in a frying
pan over high heat, stirring, for 2 minutes or until crisp.
Toss the pancetta, butter, mint and pepper with the peas
and serve immediately. Serves 4 as a side dish.

vegetable rice paper rolls

20 small rounds rice paper*
filling
100g (3 1/2 oz) rice vermicelli noodles
200g (7 oz) snow peas (mange tout)
1 carrot, peeled and shredded
1/2 cup coriander (cilantro) leaves
1/2 cup mint leaves
1/4 cup chopped unsalted peanuts
1 tablespoon soy sauce
1 tablespoon lemon juice
dipping sauce
1 tablespoon brown sugar
1/4 cup (2 fl oz) light soy sauce

To make the filling, place the noodles in a bowl of boiling
water and allow to stand for 3 minutes. Drain and set aside.
Cook the snow peas in a saucepan of boiling water
for 1 minute. Drain and cool under running water. Shred
the snow peas then combine with the noodles, carrot,
coriander, mint, peanuts, soy sauce and lemon juice.
To make the dipping sauce, stir the sugar into the soy
sauce until dissolved.
To assemble, place a rice paper round into a bowl of hot
water and soak for 10 seconds or until soft. Remove and
place on a clean tea towel. Place some filling down the
middle of the round and fold up one end.▪ Roll to enclose,
leaving the top end open. Serve with the dipping sauce.
Makes 20.
▪ For a stronger flavour, extra coriander and mint leaves
can be laid inside the rice paper when rolling.

pumpkin and goat's cheese pizza

1 quantity basic pizza dough*
semolina for dusting
topping
1.5 kg (3 lb) pumpkin, peeled and chopped
300g (10 oz) goat's cheese, crumbled
12–14 slices pancetta or prosciutto
2 tablespoons thyme leaves
olive oil

Preheat the oven to 220°C (425°F). Place the pumpkin
on a baking tray and bake for 30 minutes or until soft
and golden.
Place flat baking trays in the oven to heat. Divide the basic
dough into four. Roll out to 2–3 mm (1/8 in) thick on a
sheet of non-stick baking paper dusted with semolina.
Top each pizza base with some baked pumpkin, goat's
cheese, pancetta and thyme then drizzle over some oil.
Lift the baking paper and pizza onto the preheated baking
tray. Bake each pizza for 15 minutes or until golden and
crisp. Serves 4.

summer ratatouille

2 red capsicums (bell peppers), quartered and seeded
2 yellow capsicums (bell peppers), quartered and seeded
2 green capsicums (bell peppers), quartered and seeded
2 eggplants (aubergines), cut into wedges
olive oil for brushing
4 cloves garlic, sliced
3 zucchini (courgettes), quartered
6 roma tomatoes, chopped
1 red onion, cut into wedges
1 tablespoon oregano leaves
2 tablespoons olive oil, extra
sea salt and cracked black pepper
1/4 cup small basil leaves

Place the capsicums on a baking tray and grill (broil)
under a hot grill (broiler) for several minutes until the
skins are blackened. Place in a plastic bag, seal and allow
to cool. Peel the skins away.
Preheat the oven to 180°C (350°F). Brush the eggplants
with oil. Cook in a frying pan over medium–high heat for
2 minutes each side or until golden. Place with the roasted
capsicums, garlic, zucchini, tomato, onion and oregano in
a large baking dish and toss to combine. Spoon over the
extra oil and sprinkle with salt and pepper. Cover and bake
for 40 minutes or until soft. To serve, toss through the
basil leaves. Serves 4–6 as a side dish.

summer ratatouille

how to spinach and cheddar soufflé

1 bunch (400g/14 oz) English spinach leaves, trimmed
60g (2 oz) butter
4 tablespoons plain (all-purpose) flour
3 cups (24 fl oz) milk
4 eggs, separated
1/2 cup grated aged cheddar cheese
sea salt and cracked black pepper
butter for greasing
dry breadcrumbs for coating

Place the spinach in boiling water and remove after 1 minute. Drain. Squeeze all excess liquid from the spinach and chop.
Melt the butter in a small saucepan over medium heat. Add the flour and stir to a smooth paste.

Whisk in the milk then stir until the sauce boils and thickens. Remove from the heat and stir through the spinach, egg yolks, cheese, salt and pepper. Allow to cool to room temperature. Preheat the oven to 210°C (425°F). Grease 4 x 1 cup capacity ramekins with butter and sprinkle with dry breadcrumbs to coat. Shake out any excess.

Beat the eggwhites in the bowl of an electric mixer until soft peaks form. Gently fold one-third through the spinach mixture and then the remaining two-thirds.
Spoon the mixture into the prepared ramekins and place on a baking tray. Bake for 15 minutes or until puffed and golden. Do not open the oven while cooking. Serve immediately as a starter or side dish. Serves 4.

essential tips The ramekins are greased and coated with dry breadcrumbs to allow the soufflé to 'climb' up the sides and give the characteristic raised top. The other secret is to never open the oven while cooking a soufflé – you can tell whether a soufflé is cooked by its appearance through the oven glass (make sure your oven light is working before you begin cooking).

a nice variation Blanch* and chop 300g (10 oz) broccoli and use instead of the English spinach for a flavour variation. You can also use baby spinach leaves.

spinach and cheddar soufflé

Asian greens with oyster sauce

1 teaspoon sesame oil
1 clove garlic, chopped
2 tablespoons shredded ginger
1/4 cup (2 fl oz) oyster sauce
1/4 cup (2 fl oz) Chinese cooking wine*
1/4 cup (2 fl oz) salt-reduced soy sauce
2 tablespoons brown sugar
1 bunch (400g/14 oz) choy sum*, trimmed
1 bunch (400g/14 oz) gai larn*, trimmed

Heat the sesame oil in a small saucepan over medium heat. Add the garlic and ginger and cook for 1–2 minutes. Add the oyster sauce, cooking wine, soy sauce and sugar and simmer for 5 minutes or until slightly reduced and thickened.
Cut the bunches of greens in half (approximately 10 cm (4 in) lengths) and steam or blanch*. To serve, place the greens on a plate and spoon over the sauce. Serves 4 as a side dish.

corn cakes

2 cobs corn
4 rashers bacon, chopped
1 onion, chopped
1 cup self-raising flour
2 eggs
1/2 cup (4 fl oz) milk
1 cup grated cheddar cheese
2 tablespoons chopped flat-leaf parsley leaves
1 teaspoon baking powder
pinch sea salt

Cook the corn in a saucepan of boiling water until tender. Allow to cool. Remove the kernels from the cobs.
Cook the bacon and onion in a frying pan over medium heat for 5 minutes or until golden and crisp.
Process the flour, eggs, milk, cheese, parsley, baking powder and salt in a food processor until combined.
Add the corn kernels and process until roughly chopped. Stir through the bacon and onion mixture.
Place 2–3 tablespoons of the mixture in a hot, greased frying pan. Flatten slightly and cook for 3 minutes each side or until golden brown. Keep warm while you repeat with the remaining mixture. Serve alone or with tomato chutney (page 174). Serves 4 (makes 12).

classic tomato pizza

1 quantity basic pizza dough*
semolina for dusting
topping
4 vine-ripened tomatoes, thinly sliced
2 tablespoons oregano leaves
300g (10 oz) mozzarella, thinly sliced
3/4 cup black olives
olive oil

Preheat the oven to 220°C (425°F). Place flat baking trays in the oven to heat. Divide the dough into four.
Roll out to 2–3 mm (1/8 in) thick on a sheet of non-stick baking paper dusted with semolina.
Top each pizza base with some tomato slices, oregano, mozzarella and olives. Drizzle over some oil. Lift the baking paper and pizza onto the preheated trays. Bake each pizza for 15 minutes or until golden and crisp. Serves 4.

spinach with sesame dressing

2 bunches (800g/13/4 lb) English spinach
sesame seeds for sprinkling
dressing
1/4 cup toasted sesame seeds
2 tablespoons salt-reduced soy sauce
1/4 cup (2 fl oz) mirin*
2 teaspoons sugar
2 tablespoons water

Trim the spinach and cut into 15 cm (6 in) lengths. Place in a saucepan of boiling water and cook for 5 seconds. Drain, cool under running water, drain again and squeeze out excess water. Refrigerate until needed.
To make the dressing, use a mortar and pestle to pound the sesame seeds until finely ground. Add the soy sauce, mirin, sugar and water and grind until completely combined.
To serve, place the spinach on a plate, pour over the dressing and sprinkle over the untoasted sesame seeds. Serves 4 as a side dish.

Asian greens with oyster sauce

classic tomato pizza

corn cakes

spinach with sesame dressing

short order

oven-roasted tomatoes

grilled asparagus with balsamic butter

mixed char-grilled vegetables

short order

oven-roasted tomatoes

Place 1 kg (2 lb) halved roma tomatoes, cut-side up, on a rack in a baking dish. Drizzle with olive oil and sprinkle with cracked black pepper. Bake in a preheated 180°C (350°F) oven for 1 hour. Serve with salad leaves or as a pizza or sandwich topping.

grilled asparagus with balsamic butter

Brush 2 bunches (300g/10 oz) trimmed green asparagus with a little olive oil. Cook on a preheated medium–hot grill (broiler) for 4–5 minutes or until tender and browned. Remove and keep warm. Heat 40g (1 1/2 oz) unsalted butter in a small saucepan over low–medium heat for 3–4 minutes or until dark golden with a nutty aroma. Stir through 1 tablespoon balsamic vinegar. Spoon over asparagus, sprinkle with cracked black pepper and serve immediately.

mixed char-grilled vegetables

Slice 2 fennel bulbs, 1 orange sweet potato*, 1 red and 1 yellow capsicum (bell pepper), 1 eggplant (aubergine) and 2 zucchini (courgettes). Brush with olive oil. Preheat a char-grill (broiler) or barbecue to medium–high and cook vegetables in batches until brown and soft. Combine 1/3 cup (2 1/2 fl oz) olive oil, 2 tablespoons white wine vinegar, 2 tablespoons thyme sprigs, sea salt and cracked black pepper. Pour over the vegetables and allow to stand for 20 minutes before serving.

roasted capsicum

Quarter and seed capsicums (bell peppers) and cook on a tray under a hot grill (broiler) for several minutes until the skin is blackened. Place in a plastic bag, seal and allow to cool. Peel the skin away. Serve as part of a salad or drizzle with olive oil and serve alone sprinkled with basil leaves, sea salt and cracked black pepper.

cucumber and yoghurt

Grate 2 small Lebanese cucumbers, place in a colander and squeeze out excess liquid. Combine with 1 cup (8 fl oz) thick yoghurt, 1 crushed garlic clove, 3 tablespoons chopped mint, 1 tablespoon lemon juice, sea salt and cracked black pepper in a bowl. Serve with potato, pea and spinach curry (page 75), as a dip or with spicy foods as a cooling side dish.

baba ghanoush

Cook 2 eggplants (aubergines) on a barbecue or over a gas cooktop flame, turning occasionally, until the skins are blackened and charred. Allow to cool and remove skin. Roughly mash the flesh (about 2 3/4 cups) and process in a food processor with 1/4 cup (2 fl oz) tahini, 1 crushed garlic clove, 1 tablespoon lemon juice, sea salt and cracked black pepper until combined. With the motor running, gradually pour in 1/3 cup (2 1/2 fl oz) olive oil. Serve as a dip or with roasted vegetables.

pine nut brown butter

Heat 45g (1 1/2 oz) unsalted butter in a small saucepan over low–medium heat for 3–4 minutes or until dark golden with a nutty aroma. Stir in 2 tablespoons pine nuts. Serve spooned over 500g (1 lb) steamed green beans.

white sauce

Melt 2 tablespoons butter in a small saucepan over medium heat. Stir in 2 tablespoons plain (all-purpose) flour to make a smooth paste and cook for 1 minute until bubbling. Whisk in 2 cups (16 fl oz) milk and stir until the sauce boils and thickens. Serve with steamed or blanched vegetables such as cauliflower or broccoli. Add 1/2 cup grated cheddar or parmesan cheese to make a cheese sauce.

roasted capsicum

cucumber and yoghurt

baba ghanoush

pine nut brown butter

white sauce

roasts + simmers

inviting
succulent
satisfying

You create much more than a wonderful meal when you *cook food slowly* — you create a mood, an expectation, a longing for good company and good times. Every delicious roast you've ever eaten has fond memories that go with it, every simmered shank is savoured like *a special occasion*.

We're lucky to have inherited our love of this classic kind of food. Our eyes still light up when we recall grandma's meatloaf or our own mother's special stuffing. And now it's our turn to do our versions of their lamb roast and garlic prawns, and to create our own classics, *the dishes we'll be remembered for* — the Thai green chicken curry or trout baked in vine leaves.

But, most importantly, everyone needs to know how to roast, what to simmer and how to make a gravy, sauce and stuffing. These are *essential facts of cooking life* — because good roasts, simmers, gravies, sauces and stuffings are what make life such a *wonderful thing*.

gravy

basic gravy

pan juices from roast chicken,
  turkey, lamb, beef or pork
10–12 ice cubes
2^{1}/$_{2}$ tablespoons plain
  (all-purpose) flour
stock, wine or water (to add
  to pan juices, see below)

Remove the roasted meat or poultry from the baking dish and keep warm. Pour the pan juices into a jug with the ice cubes and allow the fat to solidify.

Skim off 2 tablespoons of the solidified fat and return to the baking dish. (Discard the remaining fat, reserving the pan juices.) Add the flour to the fat in the pan and stir over medium heat for 4–5 minutes or until the paste is a golden straw colour.

Make the pan juices in the jug up to 2 cups with the stock, wine or water. Slowly whisk the liquid into the flour mixture until a smooth consistency. Stir until the gravy boils and thickens. Makes 2 cups.

the fat ratio **Some lean cuts of meat may not yield enough fat to make the gravy; use 1 tablespoon of butter to supplement the fat content if necessary. Other types of meat, particularly some lamb and pork cuts, produce an excessive amount of fat.** the lumpy gravy dilemma **Add the liquid to the flour paste slowly to minimise the chance of lumps forming. If lumps do form, continue cooking the gravy and simply sieve it through a strainer and reheat before serving.**

lamb shanks with tomato and rosemary

Italian baked veal

roast beef fillet

lamb shanks with tomato and rosemary

8 lamb shanks, trimmed ■
plain (all-purpose) flour for coating
2 tablespoons olive oil
2 onions, sliced
4 cloves garlic, sliced
1 cup (8 fl oz) red wine
2¹/₂ cups (1 pint) beef stock
400g (14 oz) can tomatoes, lightly crushed
1 tablespoon rosemary leaves
2 tablespoons chopped flat-leaf parsley
sea salt and cracked black pepper

Toss the lamb shanks in flour, shaking off any excess. Place
half of the oil in a large, deep frying pan over high heat.
Add the shanks and brown well. Remove and set aside.
Add the remaining oil to the pan and cook the onions and
garlic until golden. Return the shanks to the pan. Add the
wine, stock, tomatoes and rosemary and bring to the boil.
Reduce the heat, cover and simmer for 1 hour.
Remove the shanks and continue to simmer the sauce,
uncovered, for 10 minutes or until reduced and thickened.
Return the shanks to the pan with the parsley, salt and
pepper. Mix through and serve with mashed potatoes.
Serves 4.
■ Ask your butcher to trim both ends of the shanks for you.
Although not essential, it makes them easier to handle and
they fit better into the pan.

Italian baked veal

8 slices prosciutto*
4 veal leg steaks, trimmed ■
1 quantity basic tomato sauce (page 148)
8 very thin slices mozzarella

Preheat the oven to 180ºC (350ºF). Wrap two slices of
prosciutto around each veal steak. Heat a non-stick frying
pan over medium–high heat and cook the steaks for
1 minute each side. Set aside.
Pour the tomato sauce into a large, greased ovenproof
dish. Place the veal steaks on the sauce and top with the
cheese slices. Bake for 15–20 minutes or until the cheese
is melted and golden. Serve immediately with steamed
green vegetables. Serves 4.
■ Chicken breast fillets, flattened slightly with a meat
mallet or rolling pin, can be substituted for the veal steaks
in this recipe.

roast beef fillet

2 kg (4 lb) beef fillet
sea salt and coarsely cracked black pepper
olive oil for brushing
1 tablespoon olive oil, extra

Trim the fat and sinew from the meat and tie with string
to secure the shape. Sprinkle some salt and pepper onto
a piece of non-stick baking paper, brush the fillet with
oil and roll it in the salt and pepper, pressing firmly until
the meat is well coated.
Preheat the oven to 180ºC (350ºF). Place a large non-stick
frying pan over high heat. Add the oil and brown the beef
fillet well on all sides. Transfer to a baking dish lined with
non-stick baking paper, place in the oven and cook for
25–35 minutes or until cooked to your liking.
Slice and serve hot or cold on sandwiches or as part of
a roast dinner with Yorkshire pudding (page 120) or
béarnaise sauce (page 120). Serves 4–6.

Chinese roast duck

1.7 kg (3¹/₂ lb) duck
5 slices orange rind
3 star anise*
1 cinnamon stick
glaze
2 tablespoons soy sauce
¹/₂ cup (4 fl oz) water
1 tablespoon honey
1 tablespoon Chinese cooking wine* or dry sherry
2 teaspoons brown sugar
¹/₄ teaspoon Chinese five-spice powder*

Wash the duck and remove any excess fat from inside the
cavity. Pat the duck dry with paper towel and prick all over.
Place in a large saucepan of boiling water for 20 seconds
then transfer to a rack in a baking tray and refrigerate for
2 hours to dry the skin.
To make the glaze, place the soy sauce in a small saucepan
over medium–high heat and simmer for 1 minute. Add
the water, honey, Chinese cooking wine, sugar and Chinese
five-spice and heat until the sugar is dissolved. Set aside.
Preheat the oven to 200ºC (400ºF). Place the orange rind,
star anise and cinnamon inside the duck and fasten the
cavity with a metal skewer. Brush the duck with the glaze
and place breast-side down on an oiled rack in a baking
tray lined with aluminium foil. Bake for 30 minutes,
brushing frequently with the glaze.
Turn the duck and brush with glaze. Cook for a further
30 minutes, brushing frequently with the glaze. Slice
and serve as part of a salad or with steamed Asian greens
and rice. Serves 4.

Chinese roast duck

roast pork loin

how to roast pork loin

1.8–2.2 kg (3¹/₂–4¹/₄ lb) loin of pork
1 quantity caramelised onion stuffing
   with sage (page 120)
oil for rubbing
sea salt
10 baby apples (350g/11¹/₂ oz)

Preheat the oven to 220°C (425°F). With the point of a sharp knife, score the skin of the pork at 1.5 cm (²/₃ in) intervals. Prepare the stuffing.

Lay the loin out flat, place the stuffing down the middle and roll up. Secure with kitchen string and rub the skin with oil and salt. Place the meat on a rack in a baking dish.

Bake for 30 minutes. Reduce the heat to 200°C (400°F) and bake for a further 30 minutes. Make a cut around the circumference of the apples, place with the pork on the baking rack and cook for a further 20 minutes or until the pork is cooked to your liking. Slice and serve with the apples. Serves 6–8.

cook it medium It isn't necessary to cook pork until it is completely dried out, as was the fashion in the past. (According to a popular old wives' tale, overcooking pork was said to guard against disease.) Try cooking your pork medium rather than well done and taste the difference.

complementary flavours Pork goes well with many flavours, including apple (either traditional apple sauce or roasted apples as shown above) and herbs such as sage, parsley, thyme and rosemary that can be placed under the pork before baking or incorporated as part of the stuffing.

crispy crackle To achieve a really crispy crackle, begin cooking the pork at a high temperature to crisp up the skin, then lower the heat to cook the meat through.

Indian lamb curry

2¹/₂ teaspoons coriander (cilantro) seeds
2¹/₂ teaspoons cumin seeds
¹/₂ teaspoon cardamom seeds
1 tablespoon oil
1 kg (2 lb) boned lamb leg or shoulder,
    cut into 3 cm (1 in) cubes
1 onion, cut into wedges
3 cloves garlic, finely chopped
1 teaspoon chilli powder
1¹/₂ cups (12 fl oz) chicken stock
¹/₃ cup (2¹/₂ fl oz) thick natural yoghurt

Place the coriander, cumin and cardamom in a frying
pan over medium heat. Cook until the spices are
fragrant and start to pop. Grind to a fine powder in
a mortar and pestle.
Place half of the oil in a large saucepan over high heat.
Brown half of the meat, remove, and repeat with the
remaining oil and meat. Remove and set aside.
Add the onion and garlic to the pan and cook for 1 minute.
Add the ground spices, chilli powder, stock, lamb and
any juices to the pan. Reduce the heat to low, cover
and simmer for 1 hour.
Remove the lid and cook for 15 minutes to reduce the
liquid. Remove the saucepan from the heat and stir
through the yoghurt. Serve on plates or in bowls with
steamed rice. Serves 4.

American-style pork ribs

2.5 kg (5 lb) American pork ribs
²/₃ cup (5 fl oz) tomato purée
1 cup brown sugar
¹/₄ cup (2 fl oz) Worcestershire sauce
1 tablespoon white wine vinegar
1¹/₂ teaspoons chilli powder
1¹/₂ teaspoons smoky paprika*
2 cloves garlic, crushed

Cut the lengths of ribs in half. Combine the tomato purée,
sugar, Worcestershire sauce, vinegar, chilli powder, paprika
and garlic in a large non-metallic bowl. Add the ribs and
coat well with marinade. Cover and refrigerate for 2 hours
or overnight, turning occasionally.
Preheat the oven to 200°C (400°F). Place the ribs on wire
racks in two baking trays, reserving the marinade. Bake
the ribs for 40 minutes, or until well browned, brushing
frequently with the marinade. Serve with crispy roast
potatoes and a green salad. Serves 4.

soy-simmered chicken

2 teaspoons sesame oil
1 tablespoon shredded ginger
¹/₄ cup (2 fl oz) soy sauce
1 tablespoon brown sugar
¹/₂ cup (4 fl oz) Chinese cooking wine* or dry sherry
2 star anise*
1 cinnamon stick
4 chicken breast fillets

Place the sesame oil, ginger, soy sauce, sugar, Chinese
cooking wine, star anise and cinnamon stick in a frying
pan over medium–low heat and bring to a simmer. Add
the chicken and cook for 6–7 minutes each side or until
cooked through. Serve on plates with the sauce from the
pan, steamed greens and rice. Serves 4.

chicken, pancetta and mushroom stew

1.6 kg (3¹/₄ lb) chicken, cut into 8 pieces, skin removed
plain (all-purpose) flour for coating
1 tablespoon olive oil
150g (5 oz) pancetta*, diced
2 leeks, sliced
2 cloves garlic, finely chopped
200g (7 oz) button mushrooms, halved
2¹/₂ cups (1 pint) chicken stock
1 cup (8 fl oz) white wine
¹/₂ cup (4 fl oz) cream
1 tablespoon chopped flat-leaf parsley
1 tablespoon chopped tarragon
sea salt and cracked black pepper

Toss the chicken pieces in flour and shake off any excess.
Place half of the oil in a large, deep frying pan over
medium heat. Add the chicken and cook until browned.
Remove and set aside.
Add the remaining oil to the pan and cook the pancetta,
leeks, garlic and mushrooms until golden. Remove and
set aside.
Combine the stock and wine in the pan. Bring to a simmer,
scraping up any brown from the base of the pan. Return
the chicken to the pan and cook, covered, for 25 minutes.
Add the pancetta, the leek, garlic and mushroom mixture,
the cream, parsley, tarragon, salt and pepper to the pan
and simmer, uncovered, for a further 5 minutes or until
reduced and thickened. Serve on plates or in bowls with
potatoes or steamed rice. Serves 4.

Indian lamb curry

soy-simmered chicken

American-style pork ribs

chicken, pancetta and mushroom stew

trout roasted in vine leaves

crispy fried chicken   Thai red beef curry

trout roasted in vine leaves

8 slices prosciutto*
milk for soaking
1/4 cup shredded lemon zest
12 stalks flat-leaf parsley
4 x 500g (1 lb) baby trout, cleaned and gutted
4 large vine leaves, rinsed and dried
olive oil
sea salt and cracked black pepper

Place the prosciutto in a shallow tray and pour over enough milk to cover it. Allow to soak for 20 minutes to remove excess salt. Drain and dry with paper towel.
Preheat the oven to 200°C (400°F). Place the lemon zest and parsley in the cavity of each trout. Wrap 2 slices of prosciutto over each fish, then cover each one with a vine leaf. Brush with oil and sprinkle with salt and pepper. Place the trout on a rack in a baking dish and bake for 20–25 minutes or until cooked through.
Place on plates with lemon wedges and serve with fried potato chips and a green salad. Serves 4.

crispy fried chicken

1.6 kg (3 1/4 lb) whole chicken, cut into 8 pieces
2 cups (16 fl oz) buttermilk
peanut oil for deep-frying
flour coating
1 1/4 cups plain (all-purpose) flour
1 teaspoon sea salt
1/2 teaspoon ground chilli
1/2 teaspoon cracked black pepper
1 1/2 teaspoons Chinese five-spice powder*

Place the chicken pieces in a bowl and pour over the buttermilk. Cover and refrigerate for 4 hours or overnight. To make the flour coating, mix the flour, salt, chilli, pepper and Chinese five-spice in a bowl. Remove the chicken from the buttermilk and shake off any excess. Toss each chicken piece in the flour coating and set aside.
Preheat the oven to 180°C (350°F). Heat the oil in a deep saucepan over medium–high heat. When hot, add the chicken pieces a few at a time and cook for 6–8 minutes or until a deep golden colour. As they are cooked, place the chicken pieces on a wire rack in a baking tray.
When all the chicken is fried, place the tray in the oven and bake for 5–10 minutes or until the chicken is cooked through. Serve hot or cold with potato salad (page 46). Serves 4.

Thai red beef curry

2 teaspoons peanut oil
1/4 cup red curry paste*
600g (20 oz) blade or round steak, trimmed and cubed
1 cup (8 fl oz) coconut cream
3/4 cup (6 fl oz) beef stock
400g (14 oz) butternut pumpkin*, trimmed and cubed
2 kaffir lime leaves*, shredded
2 tablespoons small basil leaves

Heat a large saucepan over medium–high heat. Add the oil and curry paste and cook for 1 minute or until fragrant. Add the meat and cook until browned. Add the coconut cream and stock and simmer, covered, over low heat for 30 minutes. Add the pumpkin and kaffir lime leaves and cook for 15–20 minutes or until the meat and pumpkin are tender.
Stir through the basil leaves and serve in bowls with steamed rice. Serves 4.

baked veal shanks

8 x 4cm (1 1/2 in) pieces veal shank
plain (all-purpose) flour for coating
2 tablespoons olive oil
2 leeks, thickly sliced
4 cloves garlic, sliced
1 cup (8 fl oz) white wine
3 cups (24 fl oz) chicken stock
1 tablespoon shredded lemon rind
1 tablespoon small thyme sprigs
sea salt and cracked black pepper

Preheat the oven to 180°C (350°F). Toss the shank pieces in flour and shake off any excess. Place half of the oil in a large, deep frying pan over high heat. Add the meat and cook until well browned. Transfer to a large baking dish, lining the bottom.
Add the remaining oil to the pan and cook the leeks and garlic until golden. Transfer to the baking dish with the wine, stock, lemon rind, thyme, salt and pepper. Cover the dish tightly and bake for 1 3/4 hours.
Serve the veal pieces on plates with the pan sauce and couscous or potato mash. Serves 4.

baked veal shanks

how to roast chicken

1.6 kg (3¹/₄ lb) whole chicken
1 quantity easy herb stuffing (page 120)
oil for brushing
sea salt
2 cups (16 fl oz) chicken stock

Preheat the oven to 190°C (375°F). Wash the chicken and remove any excess fat from the cavity. Pat dry with paper towel. Prepare the stuffing.

Spoon the stuffing into the cavity of the chicken, packing it loosely. Tie the legs together using kitchen string.

Place the chicken on a rack in a baking dish. Brush with oil and sprinkle with salt. Pour the stock into the base of the dish. Bake for 1 hour or until cooked through when tested with a skewer. Use the pan juices to make gravy (page 93). Serves 4.

roasting times **The larger the chicken, the longer it will take to roast. As a guide, you will need to cook a size 14 (1.4 kg/3 lb) chicken for 50–55 minutes; a size 16 (1.6 kg/3¹/₄ lb) for 1 hour; a size 18 (1.8 kg/3¹/₂ lb) for 65–70 minutes.**
is it cooked yet? **Test whether the chicken is cooked by using a meat thermometer or prick the chicken with a skewer in the thickest part – between the leg and the thigh – where the juice should run clear. If the juice is still pinkish, return the chicken to the oven for an extra 10–15 minutes and then test again.**
for a crispy skin **If you prefer your chicken with a crispy skin, don't add the stock to the base of the pan. The stock creates moisture in the heat of the oven, which keeps the chicken nice and moist but also prevents crisping of the skin.**

roast chicken

Thai green chicken curry

mint gremolata-crusted lamb racks

moussaka

Thai green chicken curry

2 teaspoons peanut oil
2–3 tablespoons green curry paste*
500g (1 lb) chicken thigh fillets, quartered
1 cup (8 fl oz) coconut cream
3/4 cup (6 fl oz) chicken stock
5 small slender eggplants (aubergines),
  cut into 2 cm (3/4 in) rounds
2 kaffir lime leaves*, shredded
1 long red chilli, seeded and finely sliced
1 bunch (250g/8 oz) snake beans, cut into 5 cm (2 in) lengths
1 cup coriander (cilantro) leaves

Place a large saucepan over medium–high heat. Add
the oil and curry paste and cook for 1 minute or until
fragrant. Add the chicken and cook until browned. Add
the coconut cream and stock and simmer, covered, over
low heat for 20 minutes. Add the eggplants, kaffir lime
leaves, chilli and beans and cook for 7–8 minutes or until
the vegetables are tender.
Stir through the coriander and serve with steamed rice.
Serves 4.

mint gremolata-crusted lamb racks

2/3 cup chopped flat-leaf parsley
2/3 cup chopped mint
1 tablespoon finely grated lemon rind
2 tablespoons salted capers*, rinsed and chopped
sea salt and cracked black pepper
1/3 cup (2 1/2 fl oz) olive oil
2 x 375g (13 oz) trimmed racks of lamb ▪

Preheat the oven to 180°C (350°F). Mix the parsley,
mint, lemon rind, capers, salt, pepper and oil until well
combined. Press the mixture onto both sides of the lamb
racks and place on a baking tray lined with non-stick
baking paper. Cook for 25–30 minutes or until the lamb
is cooked to your liking. Serve with crispy roast vegetables
or a simple salad. Serves 4.
▪ Ask your butcher to French trim* the lamb racks, which
involves removing all the fat from the bones. Although not
essential, it looks neater and means your fingers won't get
as greasy when you pick up the bones.

moussaka

1 tablespoon olive oil
2 cloves garlic, finely chopped
2 onions, chopped
1 kg (2 lb) lamb mince
700ml (24 fl oz) tomato puree
1 cup (8 fl oz) beef stock
1/2 teaspoon ground cinnamon
1/4 cup chopped mint
2 tablespoons chopped flat-leaf parsley
sea salt and cracked black pepper
3 eggplants (aubergines) (1.5 kg/3 lb), thinly sliced
olive oil, extra
1 1/2 cups grated mozzarella
1 cup grated parmesan cheese

Place a large, deep frying pan over medium heat. Add the
oil, garlic and onion and cook for 4 minutes or until soft.
Add the meat and cook for 5 minutes or until browned.
Add the tomatoes, stock, cinnamon, mint, parsley, salt and
pepper and cook for 15–20 minutes or until reduced and
thickened. Set aside to cool.
Meanwhile, sprinkle the eggplant slices with salt and set
aside for 15 minutes. Rinse and pat dry with paper towel.
Brush the eggplant lightly with oil and cook in batches in
a large non-stick frying pan over medium heat until golden.
To assemble, place one-third of the eggplant slices in
the base of a 22 cm (9 in) square ovenproof dish. Top
with one-third of the cheeses and half of the meat sauce.
Continue layering, finishing with a layer of cheese. Place
in the oven and cook for 35 minutes or until the cheese
is golden. Serve with crusty bread. Serves 4–6.

baked fish fillets with tomatoes

350g (11 1/2 oz) cherry tomatoes
1 tablespoon shredded lemon zest
8 cloves garlic, bruised
1 1/2 tablespoons salted capers*, rinsed
1/3 cup (2 1/2 fl oz) olive oil
4 x 120g (4 oz) firm white fish fillets, such as snapper
lemon juice
sea salt and cracked black pepper

Preheat the oven to 180°C (350°F). Place the tomatoes,
lemon zest, garlic and capers in a baking dish. Drizzle
with half of the oil and bake for 20 minutes.
Add the fish fillets to the baking tray, drizzle with the
remaining oil and cook for a further 15–20 minutes or
until golden and cooked through.
Drizzle with lemon juice and sprinkle with salt and pepper.
Serve with the tomatoes and a green salad. Serves 4.

baked fish fillets with tomatoes

roast leg of lamb

how to roast leg of lamb

12 pink-eye potatoes
olive oil
sea salt
2 bunches rosemary
2.5 kg (5 lb) leg of lamb, trimmed
glaze
1/4 cup seeded mustard
1/4 cup (2 fl oz) honey

Preheat the oven to 200°C (400°F). Place the potatoes in a bowl, sprinkle with oil and salt and toss to coat. Transfer to a baking dish.

Place a rack on top of the tray and place the rosemary on the rack. Place the lamb on top of the rosemary and cook for 1 hour. Meanwhile, combine the mustard and honey to make the glaze.

After 1 hour, brush the lamb with the glaze. Return it to the oven for 30 minutes, brushing once more with the glaze. Serve with the baked potatoes. Serves 4–6.

different glazing flavours **Add some crushed garlic, chopped lemon zest or chopped mint to the glaze to vary the flavour.**
a boned leg of lamb **Get your butcher to remove the bone from the lamb then stuff the cavity (choose from the stuffings on page 120) and tie with kitchen string to secure. Boned and stuffed lamb will take longer to cook than a leg with a bone in it, so extend the cooking time by 15 minutes and check for doneness with a skewer.**
butterfly and marinate **Or get your butcher to remove the bone and butterfly the lamb open to flatten it. Marinate the meat with chopped herbs, mustard and olive oil or a marinade of your liking, then cook on a barbecue or bake in the oven.**

Christmas turkey

Chinese barbecue pork

garlic prawns

Christmas turkey

4.5–5 kg (9–10 lb) turkey
2 quantities easy herb or lemon and herb stuffing (page 120)
100g (3¹/2 oz) butter, softened
4 cups (1³/4 pints) chicken stock
sea salt and cracked black pepper

Preheat the oven to 190°C (375°F). Wash the turkey and dry with paper towel. Prepare the stuffing and spoon loosely into the cavity. Tie the legs together with kitchen string. Spoon the butter between the turkey skin and breast meat to keep it tender and juicy. Sprinkle with salt and pepper and place the turkey breast-side up on a greased rack in a baking dish. Pour the stock into the base of the dish, cover the turkey with well-greased aluminium foil and cook for 1 hour.
Remove the foil and cook for another hour or until cooked when tested with a skewer. Slice into portions and serve with gravy (page 93) and baked vegetables. Serves 8–10.

Chinese barbecue pork

¹/4 cup (2 fl oz) hoisin sauce*
2 tablespoons soy sauce
¹/4 cup (2 fl oz) honey
1¹/2 tablespoons Chinese cooking wine* or dry sherry
1 teaspoon Chinese five-spice powder*
1 kg (2 lb) pork neck cut into 5cm (2 in) wide strips

Combine the hoisin sauce, soy sauce, honey, Chinese cooking wine and Chinese five-spice in a large non-metallic bowl. Add the pork pieces and mix to coat well. Cover and refrigerate for at least 3 hours or overnight.
Preheat the oven to 200°C (400°F). Drain the pork, reserving the marinade, and place on a rack in a baking dish. Bake for 40 minutes or until cooked through, brushing with marinade frequently.
Slice and serve with steamed greens and rice or add to a soup or stir-fry. Serves 4.

garlic prawns

4 tablespoons olive oil
4 tablespoons butter
8 cloves garlic, finely chopped
¹/2 teaspoon chilli flakes
24 medium green (raw) prawns (shrimp),
    peeled, tails left intact
2 teaspoons chopped flat-leaf parsley
sea salt

Heat four small pans on the stovetop over medium heat. Divide the oil, butter, garlic and chilli flakes between the pans and cook for 1 minute or until the butter melts. Reduce the heat to low. Divide the prawns, parsley and a little salt between the pans and cook for 1–2 minutes each side or until the prawns are cooked through. Serve in pans with slices of crusty fresh bread or baguette. Serves 4.

glazed ham

8 kg (16 lb) leg ham
cloves for studding
glaze
¹/2 cup (4 fl oz) fresh orange juice
¹/3 cup brown sugar
¹/4 cup Dijon mustard
¹/3 cup (2¹/2 fl oz) honey

Preheat the oven to 190°C (375°F). Remove the skin from the ham and score the fat in a diamond pattern. Stud a clove in the middle of each diamond and place the ham in a baking dish lined with several layers of non-stick baking paper.
To make the glaze, place the orange juice, sugar, mustard and honey in a small saucepan over medium heat. Simmer, stirring occasionally, for 15 minutes or until thickened. Brush the ham with the glaze and bake for 10 minutes. Glaze again and bake for another 10 minutes. Repeat and bake for a final 10 minutes. Allow the ham to stand for 5 minutes before carving. Serve with roasted vegetables or cold salads. Serves 8–10.

glazed ham

short order

Yorkshire puddings

béarnaise sauce

salsa verde

béarnaise sauce

Place 100 ml (3½ fl oz) white wine in a saucepan with 2 tablespoons white wine vinegar and 1½ tablespoons chopped tarragon. Cook over high heat for 5 minutes or until reduced to 2 tablespoons. Strain and place in a small clean saucepan. Add 3 egg yolks and whisk over low heat for 40–50 seconds or until thick and foamy; do not overcook or the eggs will scramble. Remove from the heat and gradually whisk in 125g (4 oz) melted butter, whisking well until thick and creamy. Makes ¾ cup.

salsa verde

Mix together ⅓ cup chopped flat-leaf parsley, ¼ cup chopped dill, ¼ cup chopped mint, 1½ tablespoons rinsed and chopped salted capers*, 1 teaspoon Dijon mustard, 1 crushed garlic clove, 3–4 tablespoons extra-virgin olive oil, 1 tablespoon lemon juice, sea salt and cracked black pepper until well combined. Serve with meat or fish. Makes ½ cup.

caramelised onion stuffing

Cook 4 sliced onions, 1 tablespoon oil and 1 tablespoon butter over low heat for 10 minutes or until soft and golden. Mix with 3–4 cups fresh breadcrumbs and 1 tablespoon chopped sage, thyme, oregano or rosemary. Use as a stuffing for beef, veal, lamb or chicken.

oper sauce

Cook 2 cups (16 fl oz) beef stock in a large frying pan over high heat for 10 minutes or until reduced to ⅔ cup. Reduce heat to medium. Add 1 cup (8 fl oz) cream and 3 teaspoons coarsely crushed black pepper. Simmer for 5 minutes or until thick and creamy. Makes 1 cup (8 fl oz).

asy herb stuffing

Cook 1 finely chopped onion and 2 teaspoons oil for 5 minutes. Mix with 3 cups fresh breadcrumbs, 1½ teaspoons dried mixed herbs, 30g (1 oz) soft butter, sea salt and cracked black pepper. Use as a stuffing for chicken or lamb; double the recipe for a turkey.

lemon and herb stuffing

Mix 3 cups fresh breadcrumbs, 2 teaspoons finely grated lemon rind, ¼ cup chopped mixed fresh herbs (parsley, basil, thyme, rosemary and chives), 60g (2 oz) soft butter, sea salt and cracked black pepper to combine well. Use as a stuffing for chicken, veal or lamb; double the recipe for a turkey.

red wine and mushroom sauce

Simmer 1 cup (8 fl oz) red wine and 1 cup (8 fl oz) beef stock in a small saucepan for 8–10 minutes or until reduced by half. Melt 20g (¾ oz) butter in a frying pan over medium heat and cook 4 chopped green onions (scallions), 1 tablespoon thyme leaves and 2 sliced field mushrooms for 4–5 minutes or until golden. Remove wine mixture from heat and gradually whisk in 100g (3½ oz) chopped cold butter until thick and glossy. Stir through mushroom mixture. Serve with roast beef or steaks. Makes 1 cup.

caramelised onion stuffing

pepper sauce

easy herb stuffing

lemon and herb stuffing

red wine and
mushroom sauce

essential

pasta,

indispensable

noodles

convenient

+ rice

They're like an *invincible trio* — pasta, noodles and rice. Nothing can beat them for their versatility, their desirability, their sheer and utter usefulness. They are the truly *indispensable staples of the kitchen* and you can use them to battle any meal challenge, anytime.

Team them with meat, with chicken, with vegetables, cheeses, seafood or fish. Boil them, bake them, fry them, eat them hot or cold. They come in *all shapes and kinds and sizes* — They cover all cuisines and satisfy all situations.

What I really love doing is updating my favourite old pasta, noodle and rice recipes, adjusting the flavours and adding new ingredients that give them *a contemporary edge*. This is one of the *great joys of cooking*. It's like making a new outfit for an old friend. Even though they still look great in their vintage gear, people are more likely to invite them over if they move with the times.

basic cooking rice

1¹/₂ cups long-grain or brown rice
2¹/₂ cups (1 pint) water
or
1¹/₂ cups short-grain rice
2 cups (16 fl oz) water

Place the rice and water in a large saucepan with a tight-fitting lid over medium heat.

Cook for 10–12 minutes, until tunnels form in the rice and the water is almost completely absorbed.

Remove the saucepan from the heat and set aside for 5–10 minutes with the lid on. Fluff up with a fork to separate the grains and serve. Serves 4.

lemon and herb rice Add 3 teaspoons finely grated lemon rind to the rice in step 1 above. After setting aside for 10 minutes in step 3, stir through 1 tablespoon finely chopped flat-leaf parsley leaves, 1 tablespoon finely chopped basil leaves and a pinch of salt. Serve with chicken, fish or vegetables.
coconut rice Cook the rice as directed above. After setting aside for 10 minutes, stir through ¹/₂ cup coconut milk and a pinch of salt, then fluff and serve. Serve with curries.
spiced rice Add 1 cinnamon stick and 2 bruised cardamom pods to the rice in step 1 above. Replace 1 cup of the water with 1 cup chicken or vegetable stock. Before serving, stir through ¹/₄ cup toasted slivered almonds. Serve with meats, fish or with a curry.

rigatoni with peas, asparagus and ricotta

baked chicken and pumpkin risotto

vongole pasta

rigatoni with peas, asparagus and ricotta

400g (14 oz) rigatoni
185g (6 oz) asparagus
1/3 cup (21/2 fl oz) chicken stock
21/2 cups peas (1 kg/2 lb in the pod)
200g (7 oz) fresh ricotta
2 tablespoons shredded mint
1/4 cup finely grated parmesan cheese
1 tablespoon olive oil
sea salt and cracked black pepper

Cook the pasta in a large saucepan of boiling salted water until al dente. Drain.
Place the asparagus in a saucepan of simmering water and simmer over low–medium heat for 2–3 minutes or until softened. Drain.
Bring the stock to the boil in a small saucepan over medium–high heat. Add the peas and cook, covered, for 5 minutes or until tender. Remove half the peas with a slotted spoon and set aside. Mash the remaining peas with the stock.
Toss the mashed and whole peas, asparagus, ricotta, mint and parmesan through the warm pasta. To serve, drizzle with the oil and sprinkle with salt and pepper. Serves 4.

baked chicken and pumpkin risotto

2 cups arborio or other risotto rice
5 cups (2 pints) chicken stock
60g (2 oz) butter
700g (23 oz) pumpkin, peeled and diced
olive oil
3 chicken breast fillets
1/2 cup finely grated parmesan cheese
sea salt and cracked black pepper
2 tablespoons chopped flat-leaf parsley leaves

Preheat the oven to 190°C (375°F). Place the rice, stock, butter and pumpkin in an ovenproof dish and cover tightly with a lid or aluminium foil. Bake for 30 minutes or until the rice is soft.
While the risotto is baking, add a little oil to a frying pan over medium heat and cook the chicken for 4 minutes each side or until cooked through. Allow to cool slightly, then chop.
Remove the risotto from the oven and stir the chicken, parmesan, salt, pepper and parsley through it continuously for 5 minutes, or until the risotto is creamy. Serve immediately. Serves 4.

vongole pasta

400g (14 oz) linguine
2 teaspoons olive oil
1 leek, thinly sliced
2 small red chillies, seeded and chopped
2 cloves garlic, finely chopped
1/4 cup (2 fl oz) white wine
680g (221/2 oz) bottle tomato puree
2 tablespoons chopped flat-leaf parsley leaves
1 kg (2 lb) vongole (clams), cleaned

Cook the pasta in a large saucepan of boiling salted water until al dente. Drain and keep warm.
Heat the oil in a saucepan over medium heat. Add the leek and cook for 5 minutes or until soft and golden. Add the chilli and garlic and cook for a further minute. Add the wine, tomato puree and parsley and simmer for 5–6 minutes or until reduced and slightly thickened.
While the sauce is cooking, prepare the vongole. Heat a large, deep frying pan with 1 cm (1/2 in) water to simmering and add the vongole. Cover and cook for 3 minutes or until all the shells have opened. Drain, reserving the cooking liquid, and discard any unopened vongole.
Add the cooking liquid to the tomato sauce and simmer for a further 3 minutes.
Toss the vongole with the sauce and serve on top of the pasta with grated parmesan cheese if desired. Serves 4.

spaghetti with lemon, capers and rocket

400g (14 oz) spaghetti
2 tablespoons olive oil
1/4 cup salted capers*, rinsed and drained
2 cloves garlic, chopped
2 large red chillies, seeded and sliced
2 teaspoons finely grated lemon rind
1/4 cup (2 fl oz) lemon juice
2 cups roughly chopped rocket (arugula) leaves
1/2 cup grated parmesan cheese
sea salt and cracked black pepper

Cook the pasta in a large saucepan of boiling salted water until al dente. Drain and keep warm.
Heat the oil in a frying pan over medium heat. Add the capers and garlic and cook for 1 minute. Add the chillies, lemon rind and juice and cook for 1 minute.
Toss the garlic mixture with the rocket, parmesan, salt, pepper and pasta and serve immediately. Serves 4.

spaghetti with lemon, capers and rocket

pad thai

how to pad thai

300g (10 oz) thick rice noodles*
2 1/2 tablespoons peanut oil
2 eggs, lightly beaten
1/2 teaspoon shrimp paste*
3 red chillies, chopped
3 chicken breasts, sliced
3 green onions (scallions), sliced
1/3 cup (2 1/2 fl oz) fish sauce*
1/3 cup (2 1/2 fl oz) lime juice
1 tablespoon brown sugar
1 1/2 cups beansprouts
1/4 cup coriander (cilantro) leaves
1/4 cup sliced garlic chives*
1/4 cup roasted unsalted peanuts, chopped

Place the rice noodles in a heatproof bowl and cover with boiling water. Allow to soak until softened. Drain and rinse with cold water. Add 2 teaspoons of the oil and toss to coat. Heat 1 tablespoon of oil in a wok or deep frying pan over high heat. Add the eggs, swirl around and cook until just set. Remove and set aside.

Add the remaining oil and the shrimp paste to the wok and cook for 1 minute or until fragrant. Add the chilli and chicken and cook for 3 minutes.

Add the noodles, green onions, fish sauce, lime juice and sugar and cook for 3 minutes. Toss through the beansprouts, coriander and garlic chives and serve immediately sprinkled with the peanuts. Serves 4.

Thai pork with noodles

750g (1¹/₂ lb) pork mince
1 stalk lemongrass, finely sliced
2 red chillies, seeded and chopped
1 red onion, thinly sliced
150g (5 oz) mung bean vermicelli noodles*
3 tablespoons fish sauce*
¹/₄ cup (2 fl oz) lime juice
1¹/₂ tablespoons brown sugar
¹/₃ cup mint leaves
baby cos (romaine) lettuce leaves to serve

Heat a wok or frying pan over high heat. Add the mince and cook for 5 minutes or until golden and cooked through. Place in a bowl and mix with the lemongrass, chilli and onion.
Break the noodles into short lengths and place in a heatproof bowl. Cover with boiling water and set aside for 5 minutes. Drain.
Mix the fish sauce with the lime juice and sugar until well combined. Pour over the pork. Toss the pork mixture with the noodles and mint leaves. Serve with the lettuce leaves. Serves 4.

spaghetti and meatballs

250g (8 oz) minced beef
250g (8 oz) minced pork
2 cloves garlic, chopped
1 egg
2 tablespoons finely grated parmesan cheese
¹/₂ cup fresh breadcrumbs
¹/₄ cup chopped flat-leaf parsley leaves
sea salt and cracked black pepper
400g (14 oz) spaghetti
2 teaspoons olive oil
1 quantity basic tomato sauce (page 148)
¹/₃ cup (2¹/₂ fl oz) beef stock
¹/₄ cup (2 fl oz) red wine

Combine the meats, garlic, egg, parmesan, breadcrumbs, parsley, salt and pepper in a large bowl. Shape spoonfuls of the mixture into walnut-sized balls. Place on a tray lined with non-stick baking paper. Refrigerate for 15 minutes.
Cook the pasta in a large saucepan of salted boiling water until al dente. Drain and keep warm.
Heat the oil in a non-stick frying pan over medium heat. Cook the meatballs for 4–5 minutes until browned and cooked through. Drain on paper towel.
Heat the tomato sauce, stock and wine in a large saucepan over medium heat and simmer for 4 minutes.
Toss the meatballs through the tomato sauce and place on top of the pasta in bowls. Serve sprinkled with extra parmesan if desired. Serves 4.

basic bolognese sauce

2 teaspoons olive oil
2 cloves garlic, chopped
2 onions, chopped
1 kg (2 lb) minced beef
2 x 400g (14 oz) cans tomato puree
1 cup (8 fl oz) beef stock
¹/₄ cup chopped flat-leaf parsley leaves
sea salt and cracked black pepper

Heat a deep frying pan or saucepan over high heat. Add the oil, garlic and onion and cook for 3 minutes or until just soft. Add the mince and cook, stirring, until brown. Add the tomato puree and stock and rapidly simmer for 10–15 minutes or until thickened to your liking. Stir through the parsley, salt and pepper and serve over spaghetti or use as the sauce in a lasagne (page 138). Serves 4.

fettuccine carbonara

400g (14 oz) fettuccine or pappardelle
6 rashers bacon or 300g (10 oz) smoked ham, cut into thin strips
3 green onions (scallions), sliced
4 egg yolks
¹/₂ cup (4 fl oz) cream
¹/₂ cup finely grated parmesan cheese
sea salt and cracked black pepper
2 tablespoons chopped flat-leaf parsley leaves

Cook the pasta in a large saucepan of salted boiling water until al dente. Drain and keep hot. ▪
While the pasta is cooking, heat a frying pan over medium heat. Cook the bacon and green onions for 3–4 minutes or until the bacon is crisp and golden.
Place the egg yolks, cream, parmesan, salt and pepper in a bowl and whisk well to combine.
Toss the egg mixture through the hot pasta, coating it well, then toss with the bacon mixture and parsley and serve immediately. Serves 4.
▪ It is important to keep the pasta hot after draining it because the heat of the pasta actually 'cooks' the egg mixture, which will gradually thicken and coat the pasta.

Thai pork with noodles

basic bolognese sauce

spaghetti and meatballs

fettuccine carbonara

135

mixed mushroom risotto

pasta with basil and lemon

lasagne

mixed mushroom risotto

10g (1/2 oz) dried porcini mushrooms*
1 1/2 cups (12 fl oz) boiling water
1 tablespoon olive oil
20g (1 oz) butter
1 leek, trimmed and sliced
2 cloves garlic, chopped
2 cups arborio or other risotto rice
4 cups (1 3/4 pints) beef stock
1/2 cup (4 fl oz) red wine
550g (18 1/2 oz) mixed fresh mushrooms
   (portobello, swiss brown, shiitake)
2 teaspoons olive oil, extra
sea salt and cracked black pepper
1 tablespoon chopped flat-leaf parsley leaves

Soak the dried mushrooms in the boiling water for
15 minutes. Strain, reserving the liquid, and finely slice
the mushrooms. Set aside.
Heat a large saucepan over medium heat. Cook the oil,
butter, leek and garlic for 6 minutes or until soft and
golden. Add the rice and cook, stirring to coat the grains,
for 2–3 minutes or until translucent.
While the rice is cooking, place the stock, wine and porcini
liquid in a saucepan over medium heat. Cover and bring to
a slow simmer. When the rice is translucent, add the stock
mixture 1 cup at a time, stirring continuously until each
cup of stock is absorbed and the rice is al dente (around
25–30 minutes).
While the risotto is cooking, cut any of the larger fresh
mushrooms in half or in thick slices. Heat the extra oil in
a frying pan over medium heat and cook the mushrooms
for 4–5 minutes or until tender and golden.
To serve, stir the mushrooms, salt, pepper and parsley
through the risotto. Sprinkle with parmesan cheese if
desired and serve immediately. Serves 4.

pasta with basil and lemon

400g (14 oz) angel hair pasta or linguine
1/3 cup lemon juice
2 tablespoons fruity olive oil
3/4 cup finely grated parmesan cheese
1/4 cup (2 fl oz) cream
1 egg yolk
3/4 cup basil leaves, halved lengthwise
sea salt and cracked black pepper

Cook the pasta in a large saucepan of salted boiling water
until al dente. Drain and keep warm.
Mix the lemon juice, oil, parmesan, cream and egg yolk
until well combined. Pour over the pasta and toss with
the basil, salt and pepper. Serve immediately with extra
parmesan if desired. Serves 4.

lasagne

1 quantity basic bolognese sauce (page 134)
500g (1 lb) fresh lasagne sheets
3/4 cup grated mozzarella
white sauce
80g (2 1/2 oz) butter
4 tablespoons plain (all-purpose) flour
4 cups (1 3/4 pints) milk
3/4 cup grated parmesan cheese
sea salt and cracked black pepper

Make the bolognese sauce and set aside. To make the
white sauce, place the butter in a saucepan over medium
heat and allow to melt. Add the flour and stir to a smooth
paste. Whisk in the milk and then stir until the sauce has
boiled and thickened. Stir in the parmesan and add the
salt and pepper. Set aside to cool to room temperature.
Preheat the oven to 190°C (375°F). Grease a 20 cm
(8 in) x 20 cm (8 in) square ovenproof dish and line with
some of the lasagne sheets. Thinly spread over quarter of
the basic bolognese sauce, cover with more lasagne sheets,
then spoon over quarter of the white sauce. Repeat the
layers, finishing with the white sauce. Sprinkle with the
mozzarella and bake for 25–30 minutes or until golden
brown and cooked. Serve with a simple salad. Serves 4.

basil risotto with roast tomatoes

4 vines or 24 individual cherry tomatoes
olive oil for drizzling
cracked black pepper
risotto
20g (1/2 oz) butter
1 tablespoon olive oil, extra
1 onion, chopped
2 cloves garlic, sliced
5 1/2 cups (2 1/4 pints) chicken or vegetable stock
2 cups arborio or other risotto rice
1/3 cup finely grated parmesan cheese

Preheat the oven to 180°C (350°F). Place the tomatoes
in a baking dish, drizzle with olive oil and sprinkle with
pepper. Bake for 1 hour or until soft.
To make the risotto, heat a large saucepan over
medium heat. Cook the butter, extra oil, onion and
garlic for 6–8 minutes.
Place the stock in a saucepan. Cover and bring to a slow
simmer. Add the rice to the onion, stirring for 2 minutes
or until translucent. Add the hot stock, 1 cup at a time,
stirring continuously until each cup of stock is absorbed
and the rice is al dente (around 25–30 minutes).
Stir through the parmesan and serve in bowls topped
with rough pesto (page 36) and the tomatoes and drizzle
with oil. Serves 4.

basil risotto with roast tomatoes

how to lemon and parmesan risotto

20g (³/4 oz) butter
1 tablespoon olive oil
1 onion, chopped
5¹/2 cups (2¹/4 pints) chicken or vegetable stock
2 cups arborio or other risotto rice
3 teaspoons finely grated lemon rind
¹/2 cup finely grated parmesan cheese
20g (³/4 oz) butter, extra
sea salt and cracked black pepper

Heat a large saucepan over medium heat. Add the butter, oil and onion and cook for 6–8 minutes or until soft and golden. Place the stock in a separate saucepan. Cover and bring to a slow simmer.

Add the rice and lemon rind to the onion mixture, stirring over medium heat for 2 minutes or until the rice is translucent.

Add the hot stock 1 cup at a time, stirring continuously, until each cup of stock is absorbed and the rice is al dente (around 25–30 minutes). To serve, stir through the parmesan, extra butter, salt and pepper. Serve immediately. Serves 4.

carnaroli rice **can be used instead of arborio rice to make risotto. Both have a medium, plump-looking grain and contain surface starch which, when the rice is cooked al dente in risotto, creates a cream with the stock – giving that characteristic creamy risotto finish. Good-quality carnaroli rice tends to give a much creamier finish than does arborio, but it's a matter of personal preference. There are also other rices on the market suitable for making risotto.**

lemon and parmesan risotto

spinach and ricotta cannelloni

barbecued duck and egg noodles

arancini balls

spinach and ricotta cannelloni

1 quantity basic tomato sauce (page 148) or
    500 ml (16 fl oz) readymade tomato pasta sauce
4 fresh lasagne sheets, halved lengthwise
1/2 cup finely grated parmesan cheese, extra
filling
2 bunches English spinach, trimmed
750g (1 1/2 lb) fresh ricotta
1 cup finely grated parmesan cheese
2 tablespoons chopped flat-leaf parsley leaves
1 tablespoon chopped dill
1/2 cup fresh breadcrumbs
sea salt and cracked black pepper

Preheat the oven to 180°C (350°F). To make the filling, blanch the spinach in a saucepan of boiling water for 5 seconds, then drain, squeeze out any excess moisture, and chop. Combine the spinach, ricotta, parmesan, parsley, dill, breadcrumbs, salt and pepper.
Spread one-third of the tomato sauce over the base of a greased 20 cm (8 in) x 30 cm (12 in) ovenproof dish. Lay a lasagne sheet on a flat surface, spoon on some ricotta filling and roll up. Place in the baking dish, seam-side down. Repeat with the remaining filling and sheets. Pour the remaining tomato sauce over the cannelloni, sprinkle with the extra parmesan and bake for 25–30 minutes or until heated through. Serves 4.

barbecued duck and egg noodles

1 whole Chinese barbecued duck*
375g (12 1/2 oz) fresh or dried egg noodles
2 teaspoons sesame oil
1 tablespoon grated fresh ginger
1/4 cup (2 fl oz) Chinese cooking wine* or sherry
1/4 cup (2 fl oz) hoisin sauce*
1/4 cup (2 fl oz) chicken stock
2 teaspoons sugar
1 bunch gai larn* or choy sum*, trimmed and chopped

Remove the meat from the duck, chop roughly and set aside. Place the noodles in a heatproof bowl. Cover with boiling water and set aside for 5 minutes. Drain and set aside. Heat a wok or frying pan over medium–high heat. Add the sesame oil and ginger and stir-fry for 1 minute. Add the cooking wine, hoisin sauce, stock and sugar and cook for 3 minutes or until thickened and slightly reduced. Toss through the duck meat, noodles and greens and cook until heated through and the greens are slightly wilted. Serve immediately. Serves 4.

arancini balls

1 quantity lemon and parmesan risotto (page 140), cooled
70g (2 1/4 oz) mozzarella, cut into 1 cm (1/2 in) x 2 cm (3/4 in) logs
vegetable oil for deep-frying

Take 1/3 cup of cooled risotto and mould in the palm of your hand. Place a piece of mozzarella in the middle, press the risotto over to enclose it and roll into a ball. Repeat with the remaining mixture. Refrigerate until needed. Heat the oil in a saucepan over medium heat. When hot, deep-fry the cakes for 3–4 minutes in batches until golden. Drain on paper towel.
Serve with a simple salad as a light meal. Makes 10.

paella

3 chorizo sausages* (420g/14 oz)
6 saffron threads
1 tablespoon boiling water
2 tablespoons olive oil
4 cloves garlic, chopped
2 onions, sliced
2 cups short-grain rice
400g (14 oz) can peeled tomatoes, crushed
4 cups (1 3/4 pints) fish or vegetable stock
1/2 cup (4 fl oz) white wine
1 tablespoon smoky paprika*
2 tablespoons chopped flat-leaf parsley leaves
1 cup (8 fl oz) white wine, extra
10 sprigs thyme, halved
1 kg (2 lb) vongole (clams)
24 black mussels
18 medium green (raw) prawns (850g/1 3/4 lb), shelled

Heat a large frying pan over medium heat. Cook the chorizo in two batches for 8–10 minutes or until crisp. Remove and place on paper towel.
Soak the saffron in the boiling water for 5 minutes. Heat a large, deep frying or paella pan over medium heat. Cook the oil, garlic and onions for 5 minutes or until soft. Add the rice and cook, stirring, for 2 minutes. Add the tomato, stock, wine and saffron mixture and cook, stirring occasionally, for 10 minutes or until the rice is just cooked. Stir through the paprika and parsley.
While the rice is cooking, place the extra wine and thyme in a large, deep frying pan over medium heat and bring to a simmer. Add the vongole, mussels and prawns. Cover and cook for 5 minutes, shaking the pan occasionally, until the shells have opened and the prawns are cooked.
Place the paella on plates, top with the seafood and serve with lemon wedges. Serves 6.

paella

short order

fresh tomato and basil penne

butter and parmesan linguine

basic tomato sauce

short order

fresh tomato and basil penne

Cook 400g (14 oz) penne until al dente. Drain. Combine 3 finely chopped vine-ripened tomatoes with 1/2 chopped small red onion, 2 tablespoons olive oil, 1 1/2 teaspoons sugar, 1/3 cup baby basil leaves, sea salt and cracked black pepper. Mix well to dissolve the sugar. Toss with the pasta and top with parmesan cheese. Serves 4.

butter and parmesan linguine

Cook 400g (14 oz) linguine until al dente. Drain. Melt 60g (2 oz) butter in a large, deep frying pan over low heat. Add the pasta and toss to coat. Toss through 1/2 cup grated parmesan cheese and sprinkle with cracked black pepper. Serves 4.

basic tomato sauce

Heat a large saucepan over medium heat. Cook 2 teaspoons olive oil, 2 chopped garlic cloves and 1 chopped onion for 4–5 minutes or until tender. Add 2 x 400g (14 oz) tins lightly crushed tomatoes, 3 teaspoons sugar and 1/4 cup chopped basil leaves. Simmer for 10 minutes or until thick and pulpy. Serve with pasta and add ingredients such as chicken, olives, tuna, anchovies or chilli as desired.

ricotta and herb rigatoni

Cook 400g (14 oz) rigatoni until al dente. Drain. Toss 250g (8 oz) fresh ricotta, 1/4 cup shredded basil leaves, 1/4 cup chopped flat-leaf parsley leaves and 2 tablespoons sliced black olives through the warm pasta. Sprinkle with cracked black pepper. Serves 4.

fried rice

Cook 2 cups long-grain rice in 2 1/2 cups water by absorption method (page 127). Allow to cool slightly and separate grains with a fork. Heat 2 tablespoons peanut oil in a wok or deep frying pan over high heat and cook the rice, 1 tablespoon finely chopped ginger, 3 chopped small chillies, 4 sliced green onions (scallions), 2 tablespoons chopped garlic chives* and 500g (1 lb) small green (raw) prawns and cook for 5 minutes. Sprinkle with 2 tablespoons soy sauce. Serves 4.

macaroni cheese

Cook 2 cups macaroni for 6 minutes or until al dente. Drain and return to saucepan. Add 1/2 cup (4 fl oz) cream, 3/4 cup (6 fl oz) milk and 3/4 cup grated cheddar cheese to the pan with the macaroni and stir over low heat until the cheese melts and the mixture is thick. Serves 2.

garlic, chilli and olive oil spaghetti

Cook 200g (7 oz) spaghetti until al dente. Drain. Heat 3 tablespoons good-quality olive oil in a frying pan over medium heat. Cook 2 small seeded and chopped red chillies and 2 chopped garlic cloves for 3 minutes or until fragrant. Toss through the pasta with some roughly chopped flat-leaf parsley leaves. Serves 2.

brown butter and sage fettuccine

Cook 400g (14 oz) fettuccine until al dente. Drain. Melt 100g (3 1/2 oz) unsalted butter in a large saucepan over low–medium heat. Add 1/4 cup sage leaves and continue to heat for 3–4 minutes or until the butter is dark golden and the sage is crisp. Pour the brown butter over the pasta, toss and top with the sage leaves. Serves 4.

ricotta and herb rigatoni

fried rice

macaroni cheese

garlic, chilli and olive oil spaghetti

brown butter and sage fettuccine

comforting
filling

pies + tarts

irresistible

There is nothing more likely to *make someone smile* than to be served up a fresh-from-the-oven pie. The joy of the crunch as you cut or bite into some *light and perfect pastry* is second only to the delight of seeing, smelling and tasting what lies within. Like a treasure chest that reveals mouthfuls of plump and juicy chunks of meat in a rich gravy or tender chicken pieces in a tasty sauce. Put some of the season's best vegetables in a buttery pastry case and anyone will come to the party.

I'm also a big fan of the tart and the flan. There's no lifting the lid but there is *instant appeal*. Much easier to make than rumour has it, you can put together a quick tart using basic ingredients in no time at all. They travel well, they shine at any occasion and there's really no limit to how you can fill them.

Always keep some pastry at the ready – shortcrust, filo or puff – for an instant meal that's easy, filling and *everyone's favourite.* Forget pie in the sky, get one onto your plate.

shortcrust pastry

154

basic shortcrust pastry

2 cups flour
145g (5 oz) butter
2–3 tablespoons iced water

Process the flour and butter in a food processor until the mixture resembles fine breadcrumbs.

While the motor is running, add enough iced water to form a smooth dough.

Knead very lightly then wrap the dough in plastic wrap and refrigerate for 30 minutes. When ready to use, roll out on a lightly floured surface until 3 mm (1/8 in) thick. Makes 350g (12 oz), which will line up to a 25 cm (10 in) pie dish or tart tin.

baking blind **To bake blind – to produce a crisp tart shell ready to be filled with wet ingredients – top the pastry-lined tart tin or tins with a piece of non-stick baking paper that extends past the edge of the tin. Fill with pastry weights (see Tools) or uncooked rice or beans. Place on a baking tray and bake in a preheated 180°C (350°F) oven for 10 minutes. Remove the weights and paper and bake for a further 5 minutes or until the pastry is golden.**

shepherd's pie

potato, rosemary and goat's cheese tarts

bacon and egg pies

shepherd's pie

1 tablespoon olive oil
2 onions, chopped
2 medium carrots, chopped
600g (20 oz) lamb or beef mince
2 tablespoons tomato paste
400g (14 oz) can peeled tomatoes
1 cup (8 fl oz) beef stock
1 fresh or dried bay leaf
1 sprig thyme
1 cup fresh or frozen peas
sea salt and cracked black pepper
potato mash
1 kg (2 lb) potatoes, peeled and chopped
75g (2½ oz) butter
¼ cup (2 fl oz) milk
½ cup finely grated parmesan cheese

Preheat the oven to 190°C (375°F). Heat a large saucepan over medium heat and cook the oil, onion and carrot for 5 minutes or until soft and golden. Add the mince and cook for 3 minutes or until browned. Stir through the tomato paste, tomatoes, stock, bay leaf and thyme. Cover and simmer for 15 minutes. Add the peas and simmer, uncovered, for a further 15 minutes or until all the liquid has evaporated. Add the salt and pepper and set aside. To make the mash, boil the potatoes in water until soft. Drain and mash with the butter and milk then stir through the parmesan.
Spoon the meat mixture into a 4 cup capacity ovenproof dish. Top with the mash and bake for 35 minutes or until golden brown. Serves 4–6.

potato, rosemary and goat's cheese tarts

375g (13 oz) puff pastry*
filling
4 medium waxy potatoes such as nicola, peeled
200g (7 oz) firm goat's cheese, sliced
2 tablespoons rosemary leaves
olive oil for drizzling
sea salt and cracked black pepper

To make the filling, cook the potatoes in a large saucepan of boiling water until tender. Drain, allow to cool and slice into 5 mm (¼ in) slices.
Preheat the oven to 200°C (400°F). Roll out the pastry on a lightly floured surface to 4 mm (¼ in) thick and cut into four 18 cm (7 in) x 12 cm (5 in) rectangles. Top each piece with some potato, goat's cheese and rosemary and bake for 20–25 minutes or until puffed and golden. Remove from the oven, drizzle with oil and sprinkle with salt and pepper. Serve warm with a simple green salad. Serves 4.

bacon and egg pies

375g (13 oz) puff pastry*
filling
8 rashers bacon, rind removed
½ cup grated cheddar cheese
2 teaspoons wholegrain mustard
8 eggs

Preheat the oven to 200°C (400°F). Roll out the pastry on a lightly floured surface to 3 mm (⅛ in) thick. Cut into quarters, line 4 x 1 cup capacity pie dishes and trim. Bake the bacon on a baking tray for 10 minutes or until just crisp. Drain on paper towel.
Combine the cheese and mustard and divide between the pie bases. Top the cheese with two pieces of bacon, then break two eggs over the top of each pie. Bake for 15–18 minutes or until the eggs have set and the pastry is golden. Serve warm. Serves 4.

beef and red wine pies

1 kg (2 lb) steak (chuck or blade), cut into 2 cm (¾ in) cubes
2 tablespoons olive oil
8 small pickling onions, halved
4 rashers bacon, chopped
2 cloves garlic, chopped
1½ cups (12 fl oz) red wine
2½ cups (1 pint) beef stock
1 tablespoon thyme leaves
sea salt and cracked black pepper
12 baby new potatoes, quartered
1½ tablespoons cornflour (cornstarch)
3 tablespoons water
375g (13 oz) puff pastry*
1 egg, lightly beaten

Cook half of the meat in half of the oil in a large saucepan over high heat for 4–5 minutes or until well browned. Remove from the pan. Add the remaining oil and meat, repeat and remove from the pan. Cook the onions and bacon for 3–4 minutes over medium heat. Add the garlic and cook for 1 minute. Return the meat to the pan with the wine, stock, thyme, salt and pepper. Cover, bring to the boil, then simmer, covered, for 30 minutes. Remove the lid, simmer for 15 minutes then add the potatoes and cook for 10–15 minutes or until tender.
Mix the cornflour and water to a smooth paste. Add to the meat and stir until it boils and thickens. Cool slightly. Preheat the oven to 180°C (350°F). Place the mixture in 4 x 2 cup capacity ovenproof dishes. Roll out the pastry on a lightly floured surface to 3 mm (⅛ in) thick. Cut out four pastry rounds to fit over the pie dishes. Brush the pastry with the egg and make a slit in the top. Bake for 20 minutes or until golden and puffed. Serves 4.

beef and red wine pies

meat pies

how to meat pies

1 quantity (350g/12 oz) shortcrust pastry (page 155)
375g (13 oz) puff pastry*
filling
1 tablespoon oil
2 onions, chopped
1.5 kg (3 lb) round or chuck steak, cut into 1.5 cm ($2/3$ in) cubes
1 tablespoon tomato paste
$4^{1/2}$ cups ($1^{2/3}$ pints) beef stock
1 cup (8 fl oz) red wine
1 tablespoon Worcestershire sauce
2 tablespoons cornflour (cornstarch)
$1/4$ cup (2 fl oz) water
sea salt and cracked black pepper
1 egg, lightly beaten

Preheat the oven to 180°C (350°F). To make the filling, heat the oil in a saucepan over high heat. Add the onion and cook for 2 minutes or until soft. Add the meat and cook for 5 minutes or until sealed.

Add the tomato paste, stock, wine and Worcestershire sauce to the pan and simmer, uncovered, for 1 hour or until the meat is tender. Blend the cornflour and water to a smooth paste. Add to the beef mixture and stir for 4 minutes or until the mixture has thickened and returned to a simmer. Add the salt and pepper then set aside to cool.

Roll out the shortcrust pastry on a lightly floured surface to 3 mm ($1/8$ in) thick. Cut out six pie bases (you may need to re-roll the scraps) to line 9 cm ($3^{1/2}$ in) base x 11 cm ($4^{1/4}$ in) top pie tins. Spoon in the filling. Roll out the puff pastry until 3–4 mm ($1/8$ in) thick and cut out six lids. Place on top, trim and press the edges of the pastry together. Brush the tops with the egg and make a slit in the tops. Bake for 30 minutes or until golden. Makes 6 pies.

chicken pie

smoked ham and cheddar quiche

vegetable pies

chicken pie

1 quantity (350g/12 oz) shortcrust pastry (page 155)
375g (13 oz) puff pastry*
filling
1 tablespoon oil
2 leeks, chopped
1 kg (2 lb) chicken thigh fillets, cut into 2 cm (3/4 in) cubes
3 cups (24 fl oz) chicken stock
3/4 cup (6 fl oz) dry white wine
250g (8 oz) small button mushrooms, halved
2 tablespoons chopped flat-leaf parsley
2 tablespoons cornflour (cornstarch)
1/4 cup (2 fl oz) water
sea salt and cracked black pepper
1 egg, lightly beaten

To make the filling, cook the oil and leek in a saucepan over medium–high heat for 3 minutes or until soft. Add the chicken, stock and wine. Simmer, uncovered, for 45 minutes or until tender. Add the mushrooms and parsley to the pan and cook for 5 minutes. Blend the cornflour and water to a smooth paste, add to the pan and cook, stirring, for 5 minutes or until the mixture thickens and returns to a simmer. Add the salt and pepper. Set aside to cool. Roll out the shortcrust pastry on a lightly floured surface to 3 mm (1/8 in) thick and line the base of a deep 24 cm (9½ in) pie tin. Spoon in the cooled filling. Roll out the puff pastry to 3–4 mm (1/8 in) thick. Cut a shape from the middle of the pastry as an air hole. Place the pastry top onto the pie. Trim and press the edges together to seal and brush the top with a little egg. Bake at 180°C (350°F) for 40 minutes or until golden and crisp. Serves 6.

smoked ham and cheddar quiche

1 quantity (350g/12 oz) shortcrust pastry (page 155)
filling
200g (7 oz) smoked ham, chopped
1/2 cup grated aged cheddar cheese
1 tablespoon chopped flat-leaf parsley
4 eggs
1½ cups (12 fl oz) single cream*
2 teaspoons Dijon mustard
sea salt and cracked black pepper

Preheat the oven to 180°C (350°F). Roll out the pastry on a floured surface to 3 mm (1/8 in) thick and line a 28 cm (11 in) quiche dish. Blind bake the pastry shell (page 155) and set aside to cool. Reduce the oven to 160°C (325°F). Sprinkle the tart shell with the ham, cheese and parsley. Whisk together the eggs, cream, mustard, salt and pepper. Pour over the filling in the tart shell. Bake for 40 minutes or until set. Serve warm or cold in wedges with a simple green salad. Serves 6.

vegetable pies

1 quantity (350g/12 oz) shortcrust pastry (page 155)
filling
300g (10 oz) potatoes, peeled and chopped
300g (10 oz) orange sweet potato*, peeled and chopped
300g (10 oz) butternut pumpkin*, peeled and chopped
4 field mushrooms (275g/7½ oz), quartered
1 red capsicum (bell pepper), chopped
2 zucchini (courgettes), chopped
2 tablespoons oil
sea salt and cracked black pepper
2 tablespoons chopped rosemary
300g (10 oz) fresh ricotta
3/4 cup grated cheddar cheese
1/2 cup grated parmesan cheese

Preheat the oven to 180°C (350°F). To make the filling, place the potato, sweet potato, pumpkin, mushrooms, capsicum and zucchini in a baking dish and toss with the oil, salt, pepper and rosemary. Bake for 30 minutes or until the vegetables are soft and golden. Set aside to cool. Divide the pastry into four. Roll out each portion on a lightly floured surface to 3 mm (1/8 in) thick and use it to line 4 x 1 cup capacity pie dishes, trimming away any excess pastry.
Mix the vegetables with the ricotta and cheddar, fill the pie dishes with the mixture and top with the parmesan. Bake for 35 minutes or until the pies are golden. Serves 4.

sausage rolls

1 kg (2 lb) sausage mince
2 eggs
2 cups fresh breadcrumbs
1/3 cup (2½ fl oz) Worcestershire sauce
2 tablespoons tomato paste
sea salt and cracked black pepper
500g (1 lb) or 3 ready-rolled sheets puff pastry*
2 egg yolks, lightly beaten
sesame seeds to sprinkle

Preheat the oven to 200°C (400°F). Combine the mince, eggs, breadcrumbs, Worcestershire sauce, tomato paste, salt and pepper.
Roll out the pastry to 3 mm (1/8 in) thick and cut into 12 cm (5 in) x 24 cm (10 in) pieces or cut each ready-rolled pastry sheet in half. Divide the sausage mixture into six equal portions, roll into sausage shapes and place down the centre of each piece of pastry. Roll to enclose, placing the pastry seam underneath.
Cut the sausage rolls into thirds and place on a baking tray lined with non-stick baking paper. Brush with the egg yolk and sprinkle with sesame seeds. Bake for 20–25 minutes or until golden and cooked through. Makes 18.

sausage rolls

how to free-form ratatouille tart

1 quantity (350g/12 oz) shortcrust pastry (page 155)
filling
1 head garlic, unpeeled, cut in half horizontally
2 brown onions, peeled and quartered
2 red capsicums (bell peppers), quartered
2 small eggplants (aubergines), cut into wedges
4 roma tomatoes, halved
3 zucchini (courgettes), quartered
2 tablespoons olive oil
sea salt and cracked black pepper
200g (7 oz) fetta, roughly crumbled
1 tablespoon marjoram leaves

Preheat the oven to 180°C (350°F). To make the filling, place the garlic, onions, capsicums, eggplants, tomatoes and zucchini on a large baking tray, drizzle with the oil and sprinkle with salt and pepper. Bake for 1 hour or until the vegetables are golden and slightly dried. Allow to cool then squeeze the flesh from the garlic skins and set aside.

Roll out the pastry on a lightly floured surface into a roughly 30 cm (12 in) round that is 3mm (1/8 in) thick.

Place on a baking tray, spread with the garlic and top with the vegetables, fetta and marjoram, leaving a 6 cm (2 1/2 in) border. Fold over the edges of the pastry to make a raised edge. Chill for 20 minutes. Bake for 45 minutes or until the pastry is golden and crisp.
Serve warm or cold with a simple leaf salad. Serves 6.

This type of free-form tart works well with any filling combination – including vegetables with meat or chicken – as long as the ingredients are firm. The cooked tart needs to be solid enough to be sliced for serving. When making it on a hot day, you may need to chill the tart for a longer time before cooking it.

free-form ratatouille tart

spinach and fetta pie

onion, anchovy and olive tarts

shank pies

spinach and fetta pie

8 sheets filo pastry
50g (1½ oz) butter, melted
filling
2 bunches (800g/1¾ lb) English spinach, stems removed
2 teaspoons olive oil
1 brown onion, chopped
250g (8 oz) fetta, crumbled
1 tablespoon chopped dill
4 eggs
1 cup (8 fl oz) sour cream
¼ teaspoon freshly grated nutmeg
sea salt and cracked black pepper

Preheat the oven to 180°C (350°F). Wash the spinach leaves and wilt in a large saucepan over medium heat. Transfer to a colander, press out the excess liquid, then chop.
Place the oil in a frying pan over medium heat. Cook the onion for 4 minutes or until soft.
Brush a sheet of filo with melted butter. Top with another sheet and brush with more butter. Repeat with all the pastry sheets. Place pastry in a 22 cm (8½ in) square (or similar) ovenproof dish, letting some of the pastry overhang the edges and trim any excess. Combine the spinach, onion, fetta, dill, eggs, sour cream, nutmeg, salt and pepper and pour into the pastry case. Bake for 20 minutes or until golden. Serve warm or cold. Serves 4–6.

onion, anchovy and olive tarts

375g (13 oz) puff pastry*
filling
2 tablespoons olive oil
4 brown onions, sliced
2 tablespoons balsamic vinegar
1 tablespoon brown sugar
½ cup finely grated parmesan cheese
12 anchovy fillets, drained
¼ cup halved black olives
1 tablespoon thyme leaves

Preheat the oven to 200°C (400°F). Heat a large frying pan over medium heat. Cook the oil and onions, stirring, for 10 minutes or until soft and golden. Add the vinegar and sugar and cook for 2 minutes. Set aside to cool.
Roll out the pastry on a lightly floured surface to 3 mm (⅛ in) thick. Trim to a roughly rectangular shape, 30 cm (12 in) x 34 cm (13½ in), and cut into four. Place on a greased baking tray and sprinkle with the parmesan, leaving a 1 cm (½ in) border. Top with the onion mixture, anchovies, olives and thyme. Bake for 20 minutes or until puffed and golden. Serve with a rocket (arugula) salad. Serves 4.

shank pies

4 lamb shanks, trimmed
flour for coating
1 tablespoon vegetable oil
2 onions, chopped
4 cloves garlic, peeled and halved
2½ cups (1 pint) red wine
2 cups (16 fl oz) beef stock
2 carrots, chopped
2 parsnips, chopped
1 tablespoon chopped rosemary
1 tablespoon cornflour (cornstarch)
2 tablespoons water
1 quantity (350g/12 oz) shortcrust pastry (page 155)

Coat the shanks with flour and shake off the excess. Heat the oil in a large saucepan over high heat. Cook the shanks for 3 minutes each side or until well browned. Remove and set aside. Add the onion and garlic to the pan and cook for 3 minutes or until soft. Return the shanks to the pan with the wine and stock. Cover and simmer for 1 hour. Add the carrot, parsnip and rosemary. Simmer, covered, for 20 minutes or until the shanks are tender.
Preheat the oven to 180°C (350°F). Divide the shanks and vegetables (no sauce) between 4 x 1½ cup capacity dishes. Mix the cornflour and water to a paste and stir into the sauce. Cook the sauce, stirring, until it boils and thickens. Pour over the shanks. Roll out the pastry on a lightly floured surface to 3 mm (⅛ in) thick. Cut four pastry rounds and fit over the dishes, cutting a hole for the shank bone. Bake for 20 minutes or until golden. Serves 4.

three cheese tart

8 sheets filo pastry
60g (2 oz) butter, melted
filling
500g (1 lb) fresh ricotta
2 eggs
½ cup finely grated parmesan cheese
100g (3½ oz) mild blue vein cheese, finely chopped
1 tablespoon oregano leaves
sea salt and cracked black pepper

Preheat the oven to 180°C (350°F). Brush a sheet of filo with melted butter. Top with another sheet and brush with more butter. Repeat with the remaining sheets and butter. Place the pastry into a rectangular 11 cm (4½ in) x 34 cm (13 in) tart tin with a removable base and trim any excess. To make the filling, combine the ricotta, eggs, parmesan, blue vein cheese, oregano, salt and pepper in a bowl. Spoon into the pastry shell and bake for 30 minutes or until the filling is set and golden. Serve warm or cold with a rocket (arugula) salad. Serves 6.

three cheese tart

short order

filo cups

mushy peas

tapenade twists

short order

filo cups

Cut filo pastry pieces into strips, brush with oil or melted butter and press into non-stick muffin tins. Layer filo pastry pieces around the muffin holes until 2 cm (3/4 in) thick all the way around. Bake in a preheated 170°C (330°F) oven for 15 minutes or until golden and crisp. Cool on wire racks. Spoon in a sweet or savoury tart filling of your choice.

mushy peas

Simmer 2 cups frozen peas, covered with water, in a small saucepan for 4–5 minutes. Drain and process with 35g (1 oz) unsalted butter, 2 tablespoons sour cream, sea salt and cracked black pepper in a food processor until roughly chopped. Stir through 2 teaspoons shredded mint. Serve a spoonful on top of meat pies. Makes 1 cup.

tapenade twists

Cut ready-rolled puff pastry* into 2 cm (3/4 in) wide strips. Spread one side with some tapenade and twist the pastry. Bake on a baking tray lined with non-stick baking paper in a preheated 200°C (400°F) oven for 8 minutes or until golden. Serve with drinks. Makes 20.

asparagus tarts

Roll out 375g (13 oz) puff pastry* on a lightly floured surface to 4 mm (1/4 in) thick. Cut into four 7 cm (2 3/4 in) x 17 cm (6 1/2 in) rectangles. Top with 5–6 trimmed pieces of asparagus and sprinkle with 1/2 cup grated parmesan cheese. Bake on a baking tray lined with non-stick baking paper in a preheated 180°C (350F°) oven for 25 minutes or until puffed and golden.

caramelised onion

Simmer 6 sliced onions, 2 cups (16 fl oz) white wine vinegar, 1 cup white sugar, 1 cup light brown sugar, 1/2 teaspoon cumin seeds and 1/2 teaspoon chilli flakes in a deep frying pan, uncovered, for 30 minutes or until thickened. Serve with any kind of pie. Makes 1 1/2 cups.

pastry initials and shapes

Roll out scraps of shortcrust or puff pastry* and cut into letters or shapes to place on the top of pies before cooking. Use someone's initials to personalise their pie, or bake on a nice pattern or simple message.

tomato chutney

Simmer 6 roughly chopped vine-ripened tomatoes, 1 finely chopped onion, 1 cup malt vinegar and 1/2 cup sugar in a deep frying pan, uncovered, for 25 minutes or until thickened. Add sea salt and cracked black pepper. Serve with meat or vegetable pies. Makes 2 cups.

filled filo squares

Combine 100g (3 1/2 oz) cream cheese, 130g (4 1/2 oz) goat's cheese, 1 teaspoon chopped dill and 2 teaspoons each chopped chives and parsley. Trim 10 sheets filo pastry to 30 cm (12 in) x 20 cm (8 in). Brush 5 of the filo sheets with oil, stack on top of each other and place on a baking tray lined with non-stick baking paper. Spread cheese mixture over pastry stack. Brush remaining 5 filo sheets with oil, stack and place on top of cheese layer. Score pastry into 60 small squares, sprinkle with 1/2 teaspoon sesame seeds and bake in a preheated 160°C (325°F) oven for 25–30 minutes or until golden.

asparagus tarts

caramelised onion

pastry initials

tomato chutney

filled filo squares

tools

saucepans and stockpots

saucepans Choose stainless steel saucepans with a thick base for even heat distribution and tightfitting lids for a good seal. Invest in a few saucepans of better quality rather than a set of lesser-quality ones. Have a small size for sauces, a medium size for curries and vegetables and a larger one for boiling pasta or simmering shanks.

stockpots Although not essential if you don't make your own stock, a stockpot is still useful for cooking large amounts of food.

baking dishes, trays and racks

metal baking dishes These vary in type and quality from thin aluminium to thick, heavy duty stainless steel. Choose a deep stainless steel dish if possible; it will last a lifetime and has a good, even cooking surface (which makes it ideal for making gravy in).

metal baking trays Flat metal baking trays are great all-rounders – bake cookies, biscuits and galettes on them, use them under the grill (broiler), rest ramekins on them in the oven, use them in the preparation and assembly stages of cooking.

cooling racks Not only for cooling cakes, tarts and pies, racks are used to elevate a roast in a baking dish – having the meat on a rack allows the heat to flow around the entire surface, permitting more even cooking, and prevents the meat from sitting in the fatty pan juices during roasting.

prep-ware

mixing bowls Glass, metal or ceramic, a set of mixing bowls is essential. Glass and ceramic bowls may be preferable, as there is no limit to the time acidic ingredients such as lemon juice, vinegar and tomatoes can be kept in them (acidic contents may react with a metal bowl and acquire a metallic taste).

colander Essential for draining pasta, washing spinach leaves and rinsing beans. Look for a fast-draining colander with many holes in the base. A handle is good for resting the colander over a pot or the sink.

grater I prefer a sturdy multifunctional box grater with various surfaces providing different grating options, rather than a different grater for each purpose. Choose stainless steel if possible and keep the fine surfaces clean with a small brush.

frying pans and wok

shallow frying pans Good for cooking eggs and pancakes, simmering a sauce or searing a steak. Choose a frying pan with a thick base for even cooking and an insulated handle that won't heat up during cooking. A non-stick surface will minimise the amount of oil you will need when cooking.

deep frying pans One of my favourite types of pans. Fantastic for stir-frying vegetables and making pasta sauces – just toss the pasta through in the pan. It can also double as a wok if you don't have room for both.

wok Not essential, depending on your cooking style. A wok works best on a gas flame, which heats the base and sides – essential for good stir-frying. If you only have electric hotplates, it may be easier to stir-fry in a deep frying pan. A wok is also good for deep-frying. Choose stainless steel with a wooden handle if possible and season the wok before using it.

bakeware

baking dishes Use ceramic for cooking dishes that need a more gentle heat, such as lasagne and vegetable bakes. Use metal, a much better conductor of heat, for cooking meat.

ramekins These ceramic cups are not only useful for cooking soufflés in, they can also be used for individual pies and bakes. Place ramekins on a baking tray before transferring to the oven shelf so that they are easier to handle when hot.

pie dishes Choose from metal or ceramic – metal gives a crisp, dry crust, while ceramic gives a softer one – and opt for deep dishes that will hold a generous amount of filling. A lip on the dish makes securing a pastry top much easier.

saucepans and stockpots

baking dishes, trays and racks

prep-ware

frying pans and wok

bakeware

179

measuring equipment

knives and peelers

utensils

baking tools

power tools

measuring equipment

scales Indispensable for fast and accurate weighing of ingredients. Whether digital or conventional, a simple set will do.

measuring cups Get a set that has 1 cup, 1/2 cup, 1/3 cup and 1/4 cup measures. To measure dry ingredients with accuracy, fill generously and level off with the back of a knife. Cup measures differ between countries, so check the origin of the recipe you are using. For recipes in this book, consult the conversion chart on page 187.

measuring spoons Get a simple set that has 1 tablespoon, 1 teaspoon, 1/2 teaspoon and 1/4 teaspoon measures. Level off the spoon after filling with dry ingredients for accuracy. Spoon measures differ between countries as for cup measures, see above.

measuring jugs Essential for measuring liquids. Get one that has ml (fl oz) as well as cup measures. Measure the liquid at eye level on a flat surface for accuracy.

knives and peelers

knives The three most important knives a cook can have are a small paring knife, a cook's or utility knife and a serrated edge or bread knife. All do a variety of kitchen tasks. Choose a knife that feels well weighted in your hand.

peeler A sharp vegetable peeler cuts the work of peeling a mountain of vegetables in half. Choose a good-quality peeler with a sharp blade. A wide one is good for peeling large vegetables such as pumpkin and for making vegetable ribbons.

zester My favourite tool. When removing the zest from lemons, limes and oranges, use just a little pressure so that you are only removing the outer flavour-filled zest from the fruit, not the bitter white pith.

utensils

spoons From wooden to metal to slotted, you need a variety of spoons for a variety of kitchen jobs. Keep your sweet and savoury wooden spoons separate so that the flavour of heavy spices doesn't taint a delicate custard or cake. Keep a large metal spoon for folding and serving.

whisk When you're making a light soufflé, a smooth sauce or combining eggs, a medium-size whisk with sturdy wires is a must.

tongs Essential. Use them to toss pasta, turn steaks or chicken, mix or serve a salad. A heavy duty pair will serve you well.

spatula For turning, flipping and delicately removing or serving large wedges of food, I find a long, wide spatula the best.

baking tools

rolling pin Wooden, metal, plastic or marble, with or without handles – they all do the same job. Choose one that feels comfortable.

tart tins I like a metal tart tin with fluted sides and a removable base. The fluting doubles the surface area exposed to the heat, which cooks the pastry faster. Use one for making all kinds of sweet or savoury tarts. For easy removal, place the tart base on a small bowl or wide glass and ease the fluted edge down, leaving the tart sitting on its base, ready to slice and eat.

baking weights Use these (or dry beans or rice) when blind baking pastry for a crisp base (page 155). Baking weights come as small ceramic rounds or flat metal discs. Allow to cool before storing, ready for reuse.

pastry brush Have one for sweet glazes for pies and tarts, another for roasts. Wash well and dry on a window sill after using.

non-stick baking paper Use silicon-coated baking paper to line cake tins, baking trays and baking dishes – to stop sticking and the need to scrub off baked-on foods.

power tools

blender A handy tool for puréeing soups, making a quick pesto or salsa verde. Heavy duty glass jugs are a must.

food processor Use it to make pastry, blend foods, mix cakes, make breadcrumbs, cream butter and sugar, chop anything. The best all-round power tool if you only have the room or budget for one.

glossary

arborio rice
See page 140.

beef stock
See page 13.

black mustard seeds
These seeds need to be roasted or fried to release a delicious nutty flavour in Indian and similar dishes. Remove them from the heat as soon as they pop and start to turn grey.

blanching
A cooking method used to slightly soften the texture, heighten the colour and enhance the flavour of food. It involves plunging food such as vegetables into boiling unsalted water for a few seconds or minutes, then removing it and refreshing it under cold water.

bocconcini
Fresh Italian mozzarella balls, in many sizes, usually made from cows' milk. Sold in a whey solution in delicatessens and supermarkets.

bok choy
This mildly flavoured green is also known as Chinese chard or Chinese white cabbage. Cook baby bok choy whole after washing it well. If using the larger type of bok choy, separate the leaves and trim the white stalks. Limit the cooking time so that it stays green and slightly crisp.

burghul
Also known as bulgur and made from whole wheat that has been soaked and baked to speed up cooking. Comes whole or cracked into fine, medium or coarse grains (cracked wheat). Used in Middle Eastern dishes such as tabouli.

capers
The small, deep green flower buds of the caper bush. Available packed either in brine or salt. Use salt-packed capers when possible as the texture is firmer and the flavour superior. Rinse thoroughly before use.

carnaroli
See page 140.

chicken stock
See page 13.

Chinese barbecued duck
Spiced and barbecued duck prepared in the traditional Chinese style is available from Chinese barbecue shops or Chinese food stores. See page 96 for a similar recipe.

Chinese barbecued pork
Spiced and barbecued pork prepared in the traditional Chinese style is available from Chinese barbecue shops or from Chinese food stores. See page 116 for a recipe.

Chinese broccoli
See gai larn.

Chinese cooking wine
Similar to dry sherry, Chinese cooking wine is a blend of glutinous rice, millet, a special yeast and the local spring waters of Shao Hsing, where it is made in northern China. It is used for braised Asian dishes and is sold in Asian supermarkets, often labelled 'shao hsing'.

Chinese five-spice powder
A mellow combination of cinnamon, anise pepper, star anise, clove and fennel available from most supermarkets. Great with meats, chicken and seafood.

chorizo
Firm, spicy, coarse-textured Spanish pork sausage seasoned with pepper and chillies. Available from some butchers and delicatessens.

choy sum
Asian green with small yellow flowers also known as Chinese flowering cabbage. The green leaves and slender stems are eaten steamed or lightly cooked in stir-fries.

cracked wheat
See burghul.

curry leaves
Aromatic leaves used fresh or dry to flavour Indian and South-East Asian dishes. Available from some supermarkets and Asian grocers.

cream
Pouring cream (also called single or medium cream) is referred to in this book as 'cream'; it has a butterfat content of 20–30 per cent. Thick or double cream, which is thick enough to be spoonable, has a butterfat content of 45–55 per cent.

fish sauce
An amber-coloured liquid drained from salted, fermented fish and used extensively for flavour in Thai-style cuisine. Available from supermarkets and Asian food stores.

fish stock
See page 13.

frenching
Refers to the way the meat is cut to expose the bone in lamb cuts such as cutlets, racks and shanks. The meat and fat is then cleaned away from the bones.

gai larn

Also known as Chinese broccoli or Chinese kale, gai larn is a leafy vegetable with dark green leaves, small white flowers and stout stems (the part of the plant that is most often eaten). Wash thoroughly then steam, braise, boil or stir-fry.

garlic chives

Also known as Chinese chives, these have much flatter stems and a stronger flavour than the Western chive. Trim the base end before using in Asian-style cuisines. Available from Asian grocers and some supermarkets.

green curry paste

A hot and spicy paste of ground green chillies, herbs and spices. Make your own or buy it from supermarkets or Asian food stores.

4 long green chillies
3 kaffir lime leaves*, sliced
2 teaspoons grated ginger
2 teaspoons finely grated lemon rind
1 teaspoon ground coriander (cilantro)
1 teaspoon ground cumin
¼ teaspoon ground turmeric
1 teaspoon shrimp paste*
½ teaspoon tamarind concentrate
1 lemongrass stalk, bruised and chopped
1 tablespoon chopped coriander (cilantro) root
1 cup coriander (cilantro) leaves
1 teaspoon brown sugar
2–3 tablespoons peanut oil

Place all ingredients except oil in bowl of small food processor or spice grinder. With motor running, add oil and process to a smooth paste. Store in airtight container in fridge for up to 2 weeks. Makes ½ cup.

hoisin sauce

Thick, sweet-tasting sauce made from fermented soybeans, sugar, salt and red rice and used as a cooking ingredient or dipping sauce in Chinese cuisine. Available from supermarkets and Asian food stores.

kaffir lime leaves

Fragrant leaves used crushed or shredded in Thai dishes. Available fresh (which I prefer) or dried in packets from Asian food stores and some greengrocers.

laksa paste

Purchase a good-quality laksa paste from Asian supermarkets or make your own.

6 large red chillies, seeded and chopped
2 teaspoons shrimp paste*
⅓ cup dried shrimp
2 onions, chopped
1 tablespoon grated ginger
2 stalks lemongrass, chopped
1 teaspoon ground turmeric
1 tablespoon ground cumin

Place all ingredients in blender or food processor and blend until smooth. Refrigerate for up to 2 weeks. Makes ½ cup.

matzo meal

Meal made from unleavened cracker-like bread that is traditionally eaten in Jewish communities during Passover. Used as a flour substitute. Available from Jewish delicatessens and some supermarkets.

mirin

Extremely sweet rice wine used in Japanese dishes. Available from Asian food stores. Use sweet white wine if unavailable.

noodles

bean thread noodles

Often called cellophane or glass noodles or mung bean vermicelli. Made from mung bean starch, the fine, dry strands are often sold in tied bundles. Soak them in boiling water until soft then drain well to prepare them for soups and salads.

fresh rice noodles

Available in a variety of thicknesses, including thin, thick and rolled, from the refrigerated section of Asian food stores and some supermarkets. Only use fresh noodles, a few days old at the most, and prepare by soaking in hot water for 1 minute, then drain.

rice vermicelli noodles

Fine, ready-cooked, dry noodles. Soak them in boiling water for a short time, then drain and combine with other ingredients.

pancetta

A cured and rolled Italian-style meat that is like prosciutto but less salty and with a softer texture. It adds a rich flavour when cooked and can be eaten uncooked in thin slices.

pastry

puff pastry

It is time-consuming to make, so if you want a good substitute, contact a local patisserie and order a block in advance. If using the readymade frozen supermarket variety, buy it by the block if possible, so you can roll it out to the thickness you need. If buying readymade puff pastry sheets, you may need to layer several to get the required thickness.

shortcrust pastry
See page 155.

pizza dough

1 teaspoon active dry yeast
pinch sugar
2/3 cup (5 fl oz) warm water
2 cups plain (all-purpose) flour
1 teaspoon sea salt
1 tablespoon olive oil
Place the yeast, sugar and water in a bowl. Set aside until bubbles form. Add the flour, salt and oil. Mix to form a smooth dough and knead for 10 minutes or until smooth and elastic. Place in a clean, oiled bowl, cover and allow to stand in a warm place for 20 minutes or until doubled in size. Makes 1 quantity.

porcini mushrooms

Available fresh in Europe and the UK and sold dried elsewhere, including Australia and the US. They have an almost meaty texture and earthy taste. Soak dried porcini mushrooms before using, and use the soaking liquid if desired.

prosciutto

An Italian ham that has been salted then air-dried. The paper-thin slices are eaten raw or used to flavour cooked dishes. Substitute with thinly sliced unsmoked bacon.

pumpkin

Many varieties are available, but I generally prefer these for my recipes.

butternut pumpkin

Cylindrical variety of pumpin with smooth, light yellowish skin and sweet, dry orange flesh. Use for baking, stuffing or mashing.

jap pumpkin

Has a thin skin, soft flesh and a sweetness that intensifies with cooking. Also a distinctive green-and-white striped skin and moist, bright-orange flesh.

red curry paste

A hot and spicy paste of ground red chillies, herbs and spices. Make your own or buy it in jars or bottles from supermarkets and Asian food stores.

3 small red chillies
3 cloves garlic, peeled
1 lemongrass stalk, chopped
4 green onions (scallions), chopped
1 teaspoon shrimp paste*
2 teaspoons brown sugar
3 kaffir lime leaves*, sliced
1 teaspoon finely grated lemon rind
1 teaspoon grated ginger
1/2 teaspoon tamarind concentrate
2–3 tablespoons peanut oil
Place all ingredients except oil in bowl of small food processor or spice grinder. With motor running, add oil and process until a smooth paste. Store in airtight container in fridge for up to 2 weeks. Makes 1/2 cup.

rice paper rounds

Also known as rice paper wrappers, these are transparent discs made from a ground rice and water paste. They are dipped into warm water until pliable before using. Available from Asian food stores.

salted capers

See capers.

shrimp paste

Also known as blachan, this strong-smelling paste is made from salted and fermented dried shrimps. Used in South-East Asian dishes,

it should always be fried before use. Keep it well sealed in the refrigerator. Available from Asian food stores.

smoky paprika

The smoked version of a bright red powdered spice made from a mild-tasting pepper. It has a distinctive, slightly sweet flavour. The best varieties come from Hungary and Central America. Available from delicatessens and some supermarkets.

star anise

Strong aniseed-flavoured seed cluster shaped like an eight-pointed star. Used in Asian cooking either whole or ground. Available from Asian food stores and some supermarkets.

sweet potato

Long, tuberous root available in white and red or orange fleshed varieties. The red sweet potato, also known as kumara, is sweeter and moister. Both varieties can be roasted, boiled and mashed. Although different to the yam, they can be cooked in the same way.

vegetable stock

See page 13.

Vietnamese mint

Also called laksa leaf or hot mint. It has long, narrow purple and green leaves and a bitter and pungent flavour. Available from Asian grocers.

wonton wrappers

Thin squares or rounds of dough used to enclose fillings when making dumplings in Chinese cuisine. Available fresh or frozen from Asian food stores.

conversion chart

1 teaspoon = 5 ml
1 Australian tablespoon = 20 ml
  (4 teaspoons)
1 UK tablespoon = 15 ml
  (3 teaspoons/1/2 fl oz)
1 cup = 250 ml (8 fl oz)

liquid conversions

metric	imperial	US cups
30 ml	1 fl oz	1/8 cup
60 ml	2 fl oz	1/4 cup
80 ml	2 3/4 fl oz	1/3 cup
125 ml	4 fl oz	1/2 cup
185 ml	6 fl oz	3/4 cup
250 ml	8 fl oz	1 cup
375 ml	12 fl oz	1 1/2 cups
500 ml	16 fl oz	2 cups
600 ml	20 fl oz	2 1/2 cups
750 ml	24 fl oz	3 cups
1 litre	32 fl oz	4 cups

cup measures

1 cup almond meal	110g	3 1/2 oz
1 cup breadcrumbs, fresh	50g	2 oz
1 cup sugar, brown	200g	6 1/2 oz
1 cup sugar, white	225g	7 oz
1 cup caster (superfine) sugar	225g	7 oz
1 cup cornflour (cornstarch)	100g	3 1/2 oz
1 cup flour, plain and self-raising (self-rising)	125g	4 oz
1 cup icing (confectioner's) sugar	125g	4 oz
1 cup rice flour	100g	3 1/2 oz
1 cup rice, cooked	165g	5 1/2 oz
1 cup short-grain rice, uncooked	220g	7 oz
1 cup arborio/carnaroli rice, uncooked	220g	7 oz
1 cup basmati rice, uncooked	220g	7 oz
1 cup couscous, uncooked	180g	6 oz
1 cup lentils, du puy, uncooked	220g	7 oz
1 cup lentils, red, uncooked	200g	6 1/2 oz
1 cup polenta, fine, uncooked	180g	6 oz
1 cup rolled oats, uncooked	100g	3 1/2 oz
1 cup basil leaves	45g	1 1/2 oz
1 cup coriander (cilantro) leaves	40g	1 1/4 oz
1 cup mint leaves	35g	1 1/4 oz
1 cup parsley leaves, flat-leaf	40g	1 1/4 oz
1 cup cashews, whole	150g	5 oz
1 cup cooked chicken, pork or beef, shredded	150g	5 oz
1 cup olives	175g	6 oz
1 cup parmesan cheese, finely grated	100g	3 1/2 oz
1 cup peas, frozen	170g	5 1/2 oz
1 cup soybeans, frozen	150g	5 oz

index

modern classics BOOK 2

save some voom for sweets....

The next book in the essential Donna Hay cooking series will feature the updated best of the cakes and slices, puddings, pies and tarts of our childhood, and create some irresistible new popular classics too: think good old bread and butter pudding revisited and new-look tiramisu.
The perfect companion to *modern classics book 1*, this cookbook will redefine commonsense dessert and sweet cooking with contemporary ingredients, outlook and style.

Donna Hay's *modern classics book 2* – coming to a bookstore near you in 2003.

turn simple into special every day

every day

If you want a regular dose of Donna Hay, subscribe to *donna hay* magazine for seasonal recipes, cooking tips and entertaining ideas.

Now Donna Hay is serving up food and entertaining ideas for the modern cook in her own bi-monthly magazine. Loads of recipes and inspirational eating ideas for every season from this Australian cooking icon. See overleaf to subscribe.

turn simple into special
donna hay
magazine

classic chocolate brownie

200g (6½ oz) dark chocolate, chopped
250g (8 oz) butter
1¾ cups brown sugar
4 eggs
1 cup plain (all-purpose) flour
¼ teaspoon baking powder
⅓ cup cocoa powder

Preheat the oven to 180°C (350ºF). Place the chocolate and butter in a saucepan over low heat and stir until smooth. Place the sugar, eggs, flour, baking powder, cocoa and chocolate mixture in a bowl and mix until combined.
Line the base of a 23 cm (9 in) square cake tin with non-stick baking paper. Pour in the chocolate mixture and bake for 30–35 minutes or until set. Cool in the tin and cut into small squares to serve.
Makes 24 pieces.

modern classics BOOK 2

Coming to a bookstore near you in 2003

ISBN 0732275350

there's a **donna hay** magazine for every season: subscribe now

yes, I would like **donna hay** magazine delivered **free** to my home for a 12-month period for:
- ☐ 5 issues for only $36 (RRP $39.75), a saving of 9%
- ☐ 6 issues (including the **donna hay** weddings issue) for only $45, a saving of 9%

New Zealand 5 issues $AU56 (including airfreight)/ + weddings $AU69 Overseas 5 issues $AU69 (including airfreight)/ + weddings $AU84

name Ms/Miss/Mrs/Mr
address
postcode
daytime phone ( )
e-mail

I would like to give donna hay **magazine to a friend**
name Ms/Miss/Mrs/Mr
address
postcode
daytime phone ( )
e-mail

PAYMENT
I enclose my cheque/money order payable to **donna hay** for $ _____ or please charge my:
☐ VISA ☐ MASTERCARD ☐ BANKCARD ☐ DINERS ☐ AMEX
card no ☐☐☐☐ ☐☐☐☐ ☐☐☐☐ ☐☐☐☐   expiry date: /
cardholder's name
signature

OR RING Our credit card hotline on 1300 555 591 OR POST Reply Paid 75019, Lane Cove DC, NSW 2066, no stamp required. OR ORDER ONLINE AT www.donnahay.com.au
+ For a sneak peek, go to www.donnahay.com.au

CODE LOY\0502MC

donna hay
turn simple into special